5—1

D0426179

OCEANSIDE PUBLIC LIBRARY

3 1232 00482 0413

Joining the Entrepreneurial Elite

650.1
ISA

Joining the Entrepreneurial Elite

Four Styles to Business Success

Olaf Isachsen

DAVIES-BLACK PUBLISHING
Palo Alto, California

OCEANSIDE PUBLIC LIBRARY
330 N. Coast Highway
Oceanside, CA 92054

Published by Davies-Black Publishing, an imprint of Consulting Psychologists Press, Inc., 3803 East Bayshore Road, Palo Alto, California 94303; 1-800-624-1765.

Special discounts on bulk quantities of Davies-Black Publishing books are available to corporations, professional associations, and other organizations. For details, contact the Director of Book Sales at Davies-Black Publishing, 3803 East Bayshore Road, Palo Alto, California 94303; 415-691-9123; Fax 415-988-0673.

Copyright © 1996 by Davies-Black Publishing, an imprint of Consulting Psychologists Press, Inc. All rights reserved. No part of this book may be reproduced, stored in a retrieval system, or transmitted in any form or by any means, electronic, mechanical, photocopying, recording, or otherwise, without written permission of the publisher, except in the case of brief quotations embodied in critical articles or reviews.

Excerpts in chapter 2 from *Please Understand Me* by David Keirsey and Marilyn Bates, copyright © 1984 by Prometheus Nemesis, are reprinted by permission.

99 98 97 96   10 9 8 7 6 5 4 3 2 1
Printed in the United States of America

Library of Congress Cataloging-in-Publication Data
Isachsen, Olaf
    Joining the entrepreneurial elite : four styles to business success /
Olaf Isachsen. — 1 st ed.
        p.   cm.
    Includes bibliographical references and index.
    ISBN 0-89106-090-1
    1. Entrepreneurship—Psychological aspects. 2. Success in business. I. Title.
    HB615.I83   1996
    650.1—dc20
                                                                96-19563
                                                                CIP
FIRST EDITION
First printing 1996

MAR 1 0 1997

To Sylvia
For always standing by

Contents

Foreword

The extraordinary people upon whom Olaf Isachsen bases this book are all leaders and entrepreneurs. It would be rare to meet a successful entrepreneur who was not a gifted leader as well. I make this distinction because the reverse cannot be said: All leaders are *not* entrepreneurs. In my experience, most are not.

Entrepreneurs are the shepherds of innovation. They assume the risk for a business undertaking for the sake of profit because they believe in their ideas. These ideas could be new commodities, new forms of organization, intellectual property, or enablers, such as access to new markets. No matter what form the innovation takes or how it is applied, its success is measured by its ability, once executed, to introduce new productivity into the economy without reproducing or incrementally altering something that already exists. This makes innovation more difficult than running a company in the ordinary sense. There is rarely a ready data base of best practices from which entrepreneurs may draw to solve the problems that would enable their innovations to succeed. Entrepreneurs usually have to make it up as they go along.

Innovations are carried out most often by new people leading new businesses. Eventually, entrepreneurs are faced with the fact that any singular innovation has a limited economic life because fast followers and others will compete the profits away. Is it possible, then, to feel content that the world will continue to generate these elite people we call entrepreneurs? History clearly indicates that innovation has been the primary driver of economic growth and that entrepreneurs have been the primary innovators. There is also a reasonable argument regarding whether or not free market economics could sustain capitalism, promise economic security, and succeed without perpetual regeneration of an entrepreneurial elite.

So my question is just why would anyone invest his or her own wealth, creative energy, time, and passion into endeavors that combine big risk and the factual certainty that the profits of those successful innovations and the hard work will one day be competed away. Are these unique people attracted solely to the significant levels of profit to be made during the prosperity phase of their innovation (assuming it is successful), or is there something more?

This book brings us closer to the understanding of just what entrepreneurs do to succeed, how they do it, and, importantly, why they choose such a difficult path. We learn that they are diverse in personality, behavior patterns, and beliefs. We get a sense of the broad spectrum across which innovation occurs. We find clues that suggest that the entrepreneurs in this book are intrinsically motivated by the power, spiritual energy, and psychic rewards connected with the process of making their ideas real and valuable. We find an unapologetic drive for profit, which is appropriate and is an essential factor in Olaf Isachsen's description of their successes.

The framework used in this book helps us compare the entrepreneurs' styles, values, fundamental beliefs, and behaviors. We begin to understand innovation and the mind-set of the people who make their bold ideas successful on a personal level. It helps me compare certain elements of myself to the field because I would like to know whether or not I could potentially be one of the elite. It is likely that you will wish to compare and contrast your experiences and style within this framework as well.

Perhaps this is the book that helps us decide whether or not we have the "entrepreneurial bug" and are confident enough to make the leap ourselves—whether we will be part of the elite.

R. Duane Dickson
Mercer Management

Preface

If you have already ventured out on your own or have a burning desire to be an entrepreneur of our time, then this book is for you. It has been written to help you identify your strengths and unique capabilities so you may use the fast lane to zoom past everyone else in your endeavors as a free and creative enterpriser. Indeed, this text will assist you to more clearly understand your unique entrepreneurial style and temperament.

In the American way of life, being an entrepreneur is like motherhood and apple pie. Without them, this book might not even have been written. People who have the energy and determination for entrepreneurship are both admired and envied. If you tend toward admiration, then you have an instinctive, positive, and constructive inclination toward those who are unique and independent contributors to the development, growth, and creation of wealth in our society. If, on the other hand, you are somewhat envious, you might want to put this book down, since the kind of creativity and strength required for successful entrepreneurs is usually not associated with envy.

The driving force in entrepreneurship is instinctively tied to a fascination with, and an exploration of, new ways to achieve what no one has done before. This might mean exploring new technologies, as Microsoft does, or recognizing and creating higher values within existing demand categories, as Starbucks, Carnival Cruise Lines, and Southwest Airlines have done. Others choose to invent relatively new "low-tech" concepts and products out of thin air—for example, Velcro, Post-it stickers, Coca-Cola, and Cuisinart food processors.

Although I do not know you, I do know that you have much in common with high achievers. That is why I wrote this book. Because entrepreneurs are both born and made, this book can assist you in understanding yourself and your aspirations and provide you with encouragement before you venture out into the unknown. After all, wouldn't it be useful to realize how your particular type of entrepreneurship could be sized up, packaged, and delivered? This would minimize your risk of failure and also direct your energies into areas where you are likely to perform at your best. Why waste time and effort in areas where you are not a stellar performer?

What you are about to read is neither new nor revolutionary; it is old, evolutionary, and time-tested. This book neither invents nor reinvents. It simply gives you knowledge that has been around for a long time and is used by highly successful practitioners. When you apply this knowledge, your entrepreneurial performance will start sooner and will be faster and more effective than it would be using any other available approach.

This is not a "what to do" text; rather it is about "what to be": which is, of course, the very best you possibly can. I will not repeat worn-out concepts such as goal setting, strategy formulation, and tactical maneuvering; instead I will address your unique modus operandi and discuss how your entrepreneurial style ultimately determines what kind of an entrepreneur you are or are likely to be.

There will never be anyone quite like you. Indeed, you are one of a kind. I want you to understand your greatest strengths in building the kind of enterprise in which you will be a superior performer. In order to assist you in contrasting, comparing, and exploring your unique kind of entrepreneurship, I will introduce you to a variety of highly successful individuals who have entrepreneured themselves to unparalleled success in their respective work-life niches. Each of these entrepreneurs is unique. Some were inspired by childhood dreams, others fell into entrepreneurship, sometimes overnight. They have the capacity, capability, and insatiable appetite to never give up: As expressed by the Analects of K'ung Chiu, c. 500 B.C., "A man is not successful because he hasn't failed. A man is successful because he doesn't let failure stop him." Highly successful entrepreneurs cannot and will not tolerate mediocrity. They perceive of themselves as not only the best, but also as the only ones who can perform at levels consistently exceeding previous performance.

In 1972, when I left my jobs as an academician and a practitioner within the California university system and Stanford University (and later the Kaiser companies and Wells Fargo Bank), I was amazed and fascinated by the perpetual resourcefulness and "can-do" spirit of entrepreneurs of all types and ages. They simply do not know how to give in or give up; their commitment has no boundaries and their drive to succeed propels them through the toughest of times while others fall by the roadside.

Of the twelve self-made people discussed in this book, I have been privileged to work closely with eight of them; and each one, in his or her own inimitable way, has made an indelible impression on everyone who has crossed his or her path. Perhaps most remarkable, every one of them is an ordinary person, just like you and me. Where they differ is in their refusal to abandon their beliefs. Ultimately, they know they must succeed.

Unlike other current literature on this topic, the purpose of this book is not to report on the success of self-made rich and famous people in order to admire or envy them. Rather, its focus is to allow you to embark upon a lifelong journey and to further understand your strengths and abilities so that you may join the ranks of those who ventured out on their own and made a once-in-a-lifetime contribution. There is a commonly held belief that God's gifts are unevenly distributed and the magic of entrepreneurship is reserved only for the favored few with extraordinary power, intelligence, and energy. But in this book you will meet ordinary people such as Beverly Trupp, a discontented high school teacher with no intent to become an entrepreneur, who then stumbled into an opportunity where her buried talents surfaced and led to an unparalleled success story. She is now one of the most, if not the most, successful interior decorators of new and renovated businesses and industrial complexes in America and is financially independent. On the other hand, Bob Lowe was brought up to be an entrepreneur, and he made his first million before he was eighteen years old.

My intent with this book is to open up as many doors as possible for you to become eminently successful as an entrepreneur. By the time you arrive at the last page, you will have discovered and begun to formulate specific ideas and concepts for becoming an independent self-made entrepreneur . . . if that is your choice.

Acknowledgments

This book is a labor of strong belief in and deep admiration for the work of Carl Gustav Jung, Isabel Briggs Myers, and David Keirsey. It is written more for practical than theoretical reasons. It is a blueprint for the everyday life of anyone who has the instinct and desire to become an entrepreneur. It is more "what to be" than "how to do." My ultimate objective is to describe both the inner landscape and the landscape you traverse in daily life, so you will be better prepared to achieve what you want and reach your goals and objectives with greater ease, faster, sooner, and with more sustainability than otherwise.

A heartfelt thanks goes to my two cohorts in making this text possible: Sylvia Neville and Dan Gudeman. That Dan could work with my arrogance day in and day out I will never understand. I dictated fast and furiously, and somehow Dan captured the essence of what I wanted to express. Moreover, his skills in interviewing successful entrepreneurs bring into focus how highly gifted people venture out on their own. Sylvia, tireless at all hours, has been invaluable in transferring some of my Norwegianisms into the Queen's English. Her knowledge of context, grammar, and sentence structure is second to none.

Finally, a special thanks goes to Carol Miner, who sacrificed many of her hard-earned vacation days reading, consulting, and asking the difficult questions, inevitably heightening the relevance and quality of this book.

CHAPTER ONE

THE GENIUS OF ENTREPRENEURS

There are some things
you can't learn from others.
You have to pass
through the fire.
—Norman Douglas

The playwright George Bernard Shaw said, "The reasonable man adapts himself to the world. The unreasonable one persists in trying to adapt the world to himself. Therefore, all progress depends on the unreasonable man." This is not to suggest that all entrepreneurs, by definition, are unreasonable. It is to point out that inherent in the entrepreneurial process is the ability to identify, honor, and live with diversity as a normal, everyday process.

Entrepreneurial Motivation

The hallmark of an entrepreneur is a never-ending desire to improve, along with an abiding interest in learning all he or she is capable of in the surrounding world. Moreover, entrepreneurs stay focused on one or two issues of importance long enough to begin to achieve the desired results. They know they cannot be all things to all people, and their strength comes from being highly focused, particularly during critical moments. Entrepreneurs also have another thing in common: They are deeply committed to contribute from their personal and unique perspective. They realize that those who profit from the status quo and "business as usual" cannot and will not champion their entrepreneurial course and indeed may turn out to be among their greatest enemies.

Entrepreneurs have an unusual capacity to thrive on challenges during periods of uncertainty. Moreover, they have the belief that although they cannot consistently control certain events, they can take advantage of those events and adapt to change faster, deeper, and more comprehensively than highly established competitors. They experience others as incapable of seeing opportunities, and for all intents and purposes, others have no opportunities. In the final analysis, entrepreneurship is a journey of discovery, the focus of which is not necessarily to seek new landscapes but to alter the perceptions and the view of what is known.

Freedom is the lifeblood of entrepreneurs; freedom means increased options. Entrepreneurs cannot be creative and content while shaping the future if inhibited by the limitations of what is known. Therefore, they are natural, hopeful risktakers, at times unable or even unwilling to comprehend the downside of their actions. Even the most conservative and well-organized entrepreneurs can be persuaded that with enough creativity, the risk eventually will be reduced.

Entrepreneurs who are able to sustain their momentum know the road to success is always under construction. They leave an impression of forever arriving but never quite reaching their goal. They cannot live any other way: They are always reaching out for the next challenge. Think of them as in a constant state of transition in which the journey itself is the goal. Moreover, they don't really want to arrive because then it is all over—and what do they do next?

Much has been written about the notion that background determines expectations. There is no conclusive evidence suggesting that to be a successful entrepreneur, an individual needs to emerge from a predetermined set of circumstances. To the contrary: Individuals become successful entrepreneurs when content and timing coalesce. This does not mean that you must be at one with the environment and experience no conflict. Rather the moment of truth occurs when there is an opportunity for transformation. And although the milieu you came from provided you with a set of values and beliefs that will be part of your persona for life, as you will discover, some of the entrepreneurs in this book were born and brought up to believe they would be entrepreneurs, whereas others slipped into entrepreneurial gear by happenstance.

I not only believe that a person such as yourself, reading this book at this very moment, can be an entrepreneur: I *know* you can if you want to. To understand your brand of entrepreneurship is critical. If the assumptions you make about your capacity and capability are out of sync with the realities of how you perform at your best, your chances for failure are at least quadrupled.

The inevitable question, Are entrepreneurs born or made? is incorrectly framed, for you will begin to discover that they are both born *and* made. Indeed, some people become entrepreneurs because of the early beliefs they acquire and develop about themselves. Others stumble or fall into situations that allow them to soar as self-made individuals. A more useful question would be, Where do the entrepreneurs get it from? The answer is: They don't get it, they have it. They have it, however, for reasons neither adequately understood nor sufficiently explained.

More often than not, successful entrepreneurs are givers and not takers of positive energy. They also have the ability to reach out to people both within and outside of the organization with the same intensity and with the intent to establish relationships. Such abilities propel their enterprise toward superior performance faster than any competitor. These individuals have learned that it is more important to understand than to be understood. That, however, is not to suggest that highly accomplished entrepreneurs arbitrarily waste time talking. In fact, their strengths are that they are highly focused and that they convey a sense of urgency when going about their everyday tasks.

Especially in the beginning stages of their respective organizations, entrepreneurs explicitly or implicitly direct their energy and attention into areas where they are at their best and then surround themselves with people who can complement them with additional kinds of expertise and skill. They know this: Force is never the remedy. They know the organization will not endure, much less grow, if people are not allowed to contribute within the realm of their own free will. Indeed, these entrepreneurs know that they cannot motivate people. They carry a hope and a commitment to themselves and put immense effort into creating a set of conditions under which people will want to deliver superior performance.

It is interesting to note that entrepreneurs seldom fall ill and are certainly not hypochondriacs. They are so devoted to their cause, their people, their goals, and their work situation that they don't allow illness to enter into the equation.

Although not all entrepreneurs start their entities with a master plan, a vision for what the enterprise can become soon emerges. Also, through the school of hard knocks, they learn that becoming number one is easier than staying number one. In the process of growing their organizations, these entrepreneurs seem to have omniscient vision and an ability to pay attention to everything, while at the same time understanding and following through with their priorities (see "The Ten Commandments for Fearless Entrepreneurs" on the following page). They strive not only to be the best, they also want to be the only one doing what they do. Initially unable to fully express their insights, they are all too often misunderstood. Then, when clients and customers see the finished product, they take it for granted. In other words, entrepreneurship involves understanding what does not exist and then creating a new context that customers and clients come to comprehend. Think for instance of prepackaged salad, laser surgery, price scanners, and airbags—examples of anticipating demand for previously nonexistent products.

For entrepreneurs, where the organization is going is more important than where it is coming from. It is important to realize that as long as entrepreneurs remain on the cutting edge and open to new ideas and concepts, the opportunity to improve is always available. It is when the assumption base in planning becomes frozen in tradition that the organization begins to falter.

Ultimately, it is the entrepreneurs' intellectual capacity that determines how their enterprises will be positioned and whether it will gain strength in the marketplace. Successful entrepreneurs can create a surprise that everyone can use. In other words, they have the ability to reconceptualize, thus changing, strengthening, and increasing the value of an industry segment over time. For example, automobiles today are not only relatively inexpensive, they are also better. The watch industry has materially changed with the introduction of the quartz watch, providing a product of equal reliability at a frac-

The Ten Commandments
for Fearless Entrepreneurs

1 You are in charge of your destiny. No excuses allowed.

2 You are a nonconformist who is able to both stand alone and be with people.

3 You progress beyond the local, the provincial, the familiar, the tried and true.

4 You identify essential priorities and avoid time-consuming trifles.

5 In your world, insurmountable obstacles do not exist; rather, you engage creativity to overcome challenges and temporary setbacks.

6 The harder you work, the more energy you generate.

7 Your devotion and passion allow you to move beyond the confines of yourself.

8 You arrive at the future first, due in part to the fact that your primary and ongoing competition is with yourself.

9 You have the ability to sustain intense focus on one or two items for long periods of time, excluding everything else.

10 Failure is not in your vocabulary; rather, you convert all working experiences, be they positive or negative, into fuel for future success.

tion of the cost. The retail banking industry is changed forever with the introduction of automated teller machines (ATMs). These are inventions of entrepreneurial geniuses who broke the rules and the commonly accepted conceptual frameworks of their respective industries; they leapfrogged the competition by conceiving products that had never existed before. As one of the contributors to this text said, "My imagination is more important than my knowledge."

When entrepreneurs are on a roll, they are unstoppable and often prepared to lose everything, driven by their obsession to achieve their goals and objectives. They have temporarily departed from the rest of the world in order to accomplish what for them is vital. The entrepreneurs in this book have all gone through several stages in their lives where, after accomplishing what they set out to do, their internal landscape changed forever. They redirected their values from being fanatical and insulated to being at peace with themselves serving the organizations they created. What they all have in common is the ability to create exceptional value, to receive recognition and admiration for their professional contribution, and above all, to be loved and admired by the people with whom they have worked and who have shared the creation and success of the entrepreneurial enterprise.

Discovering Your Brand of Entrepreneurship

All too often, people at work spend inordinate time belaboring their weaknesses and attempting to improve their performance in areas where they will never shine. But highly successful entrepreneurs discover their strengths, learn to build on them, and over time attract others who complement their unique capabilities. This environment not only sustains itself but dramatically outperforms competition.

Assume for a moment you find yourself in a situation where you have the opportunity to build a business. The opportunity could emerge from an incomplete concept; it could emerge from a dream and an idea whose time has come; it could present a chance to excel within a known technology; or it could arise from ongoing development and growth of an existing enterprise. Here are four distinct entrepreneurial scenarios:

1. Continue to build an existing enterprise with a known industry or practice. The strength in this particular kind of entrepreneurship is reflected in *administrating* within the disciplined framework of routines.
2. Deliver spectacular performance within a known technology. This kind of entrepreneur derives great satisfaction from fast *tactical* decisions that impress people with the particular kind of genius behind the decisions.
3. Realize a to-be-completed concept. The entrepreneur who thrives in this environment tends to be highly *strategic* and fascinated by incomplete concepts, and approaches work through a strong reasoning power.
4. Turn a dream or an idea into an enterprise. The entrepreneur who is a strong contributor in this work environment values *idealism*, mutuality, and a strong sense of meaningfulness at work.

If your choice is to pursue the first opportunity—to grow an existing enterprise—your brand of entrepreneurship is one of enjoying the responsibility of taking an organization into the future by realizing its potential using the available financial, human, and physical resources. In chapter 3, you will meet Andre Staffelbach, an entrepreneur who has been such for the past thirty years and who is one of the most respected interior designer/interior architects in the United States. If building an organization is your proclivity, you are a consensus person who strives to bring out the best both in people and in the total situation. Your comfort zone as an entrepreneur is to assume the role of the Administrator.

If you are the kind of person who is excited by spur-of-the-moment opportunities, you may be a high-flying risktaker eyeing territories where no one previously has ventured. That is not to suggest that you fly half-cocked; rather, you are capable of understanding the immediate value of an opportunity. David Tieger, one of the most accomplished and modest entrepreneurs in America, has the competence and capability to turn failing organizations into new realms. He and his key people have set the standard in how to grow a state-of-the-art management consulting firm. You, like David, are also likely to be a perfectionist, and you can be thought of as the Tactician.

If your choice is to pursue the third opportunity—bringing into reality a to-be-actualized concept or idea—you are the type of entrepreneur who prefers to be challenged by transforming the unknown into reality. You are inclined to be strategic in your approach and content to deal with abstractions rather than to focus on routine day-to-day situations. Indeed, what you bring into an entrepreneurial situation is a vision of how to arrive at the future first. Moreover, you are likely to put yourself in a position where your success is dependent mainly upon yourself and a few other intellectually capable individuals. You are an independent free thinker and not necessarily much of a collaborator. Ultimately, the challenge will be to translate your vision into reality, and you may find yourself deriving more satisfaction from ideas than from mundane routine. A sense of urgency may well prevail, for you know that by the time the rules of the road are known, the traffic in the fast lane of opportunity is slowing down, and it's too late to be the first to arrive. Indeed, you could be regarded as the Strategist.

Finally, if you come together with others to realize a dream or work for a worthwhile cause, creating value for the benefit of people, then your style of entrepreneurship is much different. You are likely to thrive on harmonious relationships. You are driven less by economics and more by a desire to deliver product and services of lasting benefit for the end user. Your passion is directed more toward creating quality and long-term satisfaction than gaining immediate financial gratification. Walt Whitman spoke for you when he wrote: "You will hardly know I was there, but I will bring good health to you nevertheless." So for you, having compassion for the people within your organization as well as the people you serve as customers and clients is imperative. You are recognized as the Idealist.

Linking Entrepreneurial Style to Personality Temperament

The Swiss psychologist Carl Gustav Jung, observed that, irrespective of similarities among human beings, there are also distinct personality differences or preferences within the human family. For example, individuals naturally tend to be either more *extroverted* or more *introverted*. Secondly, they gather information, predominantly relying either upon their *sensing* or *intuitive* capabilities. Sensing means utilizing the senses and being alert to the concrete and tangible. An intuitive person is abstract and inclined to sacrifice the here and now for future rewards. Thirdly, people process information either through *feeling* or *thinking*. In the 1950s, two Americans, Katharine C. Briggs and her daughter, Isabel Briggs Myers, added a fourth dimension—that of *judging* and *perceiving*—indicators of how one arranges the gathered and processed information. The judging individual is quite structured, whereas the perceiving individual is spontaneous, open, and unstructured.

Based on the work of Jung, Briggs, Myers, and David Keirsey, your personality temperament can be categorized as:

1. A concrete affiliator or what Jung called a *sensing judging* person. You rely upon your senses and you organize by exercising judgments. You are an *Administrator*.

2. A concrete pragmatist or what may be called a *sensing perceiver*. You gather information through your senses and organize it through your perceptive preferences. You are a *Tactician*.

3. An abstract pragmatist or what may be called an *intuitive thinker*. In other words, you rely upon your ability to reason combined with the use of your intuition. You are a *Strategist*.

4. An abstract affiliator or what may be called an *intuitive feeler*. You rely upon your values and intuition. You are an *Idealist*.

What is *your* entrepreneurial style? The best way to answer this question would be to use an instrument such as the *Myers-Briggs Type Indicator®* to discover your personality style in terms of the descriptions defined above. However, for the sake of expediency and simplicity, we have included a short questionnaire on the following page to help you identify which one of the four entrepreneurial styles best describes you. I encourage you to answer these items before proceeding with the descriptions that follow.

What Is Your *Entrepreneurial* Style?

Enter a 0 or 1 depending on the word phrase that most accurately describes your preference or behavior. If both equally apply, choose the one that you would prefer to live by.

SECTION ONE

0	1	Enter 0 or 1
Doer—on the go	Reflective and meditative	
Concrete	Abstract	
What is real	What can become	
Trust what you clearly see, smell, touch, feel, and hear	Trust what appears to be	
Specific	Theoretical	
Act first and think later	Think first and act later	
Require and produce immediate results	Visionary and idealistic	

Add up the points for each response and enter it here. ⟶ **TOTAL** [_____]

If the total points were 0 to 3, then go to section two.
If the total points were 4 to 7, then go to section three.

SECTION TWO

0	1	Enter 0 or 1
Structured and organized	Spontaneous and adaptive	
Decisions are necessary	Decisions can wait or be changed	
It's important to be on time	It's important to respond to what comes up	
Irritated when distracted	Willing to accommodate when distracted	
Get things done—now	Keep things going	
The goal is the priority	Process is important	
Closure	Options	

Add up the points for each response and enter it here. ⟶ **TOTAL** [_____]

If the total points were 0 to 3, then you are an **Administrator.**
If the total points were 4 to 7, then you are a **Tactician.**

SECTION THREE

0	1	Enter 0 or 1
Focus on facts	Focus on people	
Resist crying	Shed tears easily	
Objective	Personal	
Consider facts first	Consider human element first	
Analytical	Empathetic	
Rely on criteria (guidelines)	Rely on values	
Consider tasks prior to people	Consider people prior to task	

Add up the points for each response and enter it here. ⟶ **TOTAL** [_____]

If the total points were 0 to 3, then you are a **Strategist.**
If the total points were 4 to 7, then you are an **Idealist.**

Copyright © 1991 by Dan Gudeman, M. S., and the Institute for Management Development, Inc. Used with permission.

The Administrator

If your entrepreneurial bent is toward the Administrator, here is how you would tend to function in an entrepreneurial role.

You are somewhat of a salt-of-the-earth type. You are always conscientious, and your word is your bond. Indeed, you are at your best when allowed to operate within known parameters, and your need for abrupt changes is minimal at worst, or nonexistent at best. Your working style is neither flamboyant nor trendy.

You are probably a workaholic and have a real sense of family in everything you undertake, be it in your personal or professional life. You like things to be orderly and predictable; therefore you are inclined to trust clearly defined hierarchical operational roles and working tools such as budgets, together with instruments (be they manual or electronic) that allow you to monitor progress in accordance with an outlined plan. Your sense of responsibility reaches out beyond the day-to-day operations of your enterprise because you feel obligated to those who entrust their working lives to you.

Social status is an important part of your well-being. You enjoy being recognized for your willingness to serve in areas where you can make a contribution, both within your industry and within society at large. You are also a traditionalist, honoring institutional practices and suspicious of untested and unproven ideas and concepts. You prefer to work with the probabilities of the known. As a matter of fact, you tend to worry, and in the back of your mind you prepare for the worst.

As an entrepreneur, you are more comfortable if you are allowed to refine, improve, and develop known technologies, products, and services. In other words, you are likely to view anything that is revolutionary, new, and promising with a great deal of healthy skepticism. You prefer to build your business on proven fundamentals and to provide stability for those for whom you have responsibility. You derive a sense of comfort from positive cash flow, money in the bank, and a steady, dependable, and moderate growth. A team player, you place more faith in the entire team's potential than in individual brilliance.

The Tactician

As a Tactician, you have a particular gift for understanding opportunities as they present themselves; you "know it when you see it," as opposed to being a strategic designer of abstract concepts and ideas.

For you, to have freedom and act on impulse is critically important because you do not want to be tied down to organizational hierarchies, systems, and procedures. You have an intense and enduring need for action. Although you might try to resist it, you enjoy your effect on others, and your knack for taking action causes your enterprise to thrive. You are a born risktaker, who sometimes acts first and thinks afterwards, and there are probably times in your life when you wish you had reversed the process.

You tend to live life for all it is worth without worrying about saving for a rainy day. In your work as well as in any other situation, life is to be enjoyed because tomorrow may never come. As a result, you are not likely to take yourself too seriously; you are more playful than other people.

Unlike other entrepreneurs, you are very much a "hands-on" type; you like to involve yourself sometimes to the point of micromanagement, to be certain that your products and services are as perfect as possible. You abhor routine, and boredom can quickly set in if your working days become repetitive. Not surprisingly, therefore, you are at your very best when there is a crisis, and you rely upon your natural instinct to elegantly solve problems. Indeed, from time to time you create little crisis situations so you can really enjoy life.

In everything you do you are a virtuoso, and you are always alert for opportunities to hone your skills and develop variations on themes you know well. The flip side of this strength is that you are not particularly conceptual. Coupled with your need for action, you may from time to time find yourself in a situation where you are not open for new ideas and thereby experience more competitive pressures. You have a real sense of fraternity, and you are probably known as the type to give people the shirt off your back. In your work, it is more important for you to perform well and demonstrate your skills as a problem solver par excellence than to make a lot of money. You are usually a lot of fun to be around and have an unerring sense of humor. You also have a hunting instinct, and for that reason you are willing to live with whatever discomfort it takes to achieve what you set out to accomplish. You probably have a sizable ego and find it difficult to be submissive.

The Strategist

Most entrepreneurs tend to be of your kind, for two reasons: (1) You are fiercely independent and have great faith, be it realistic or unrealistic, in the promise of the future. As a matter of fact, you tend to live your life in the future and you have neither the interest nor the time to consider the everyday chores of a business; and (2) you are unusually conceptual in your approach and you have an insatiable need to know why things are the way they are. You always challenge yourself intellectually to go one step further in exploring and understanding the realm of new possibilities.

You can also be an intellectual snob or dilettante, and there may be times when people experience you as arrogant. Clearly, that is not your intent, but what is obvious for you is often not in focus for others. You are also highly critical and are usually open to learning as much as you can about yourself. You do not suffer fools gladly, and you believe that the worst label that could be put on you is that you are incompetent. More often than not, nothing is ever complete in your world of work. Your associates probably experience you as constantly facing a moving target. Your mind is seldom, if ever, at rest and you tend to work hard at everything you do.

As an entrepreneur, you tend to be highly competitive, and the person you enjoy competing with the most is yourself. You are self-sufficient, and if you tell people you are a great team player, you are probably not telling the whole truth. You may from time to time play with the team, but you are far too independent to rely on it for your own success.

You have a great need for power—over nature. You always need to find answers where your knowledge is limited, and when you know, you get bored and turn to the next batch of uncertainty. You tend to think in categorical terms in order to simplify and classify issues so that you can be highly efficient; you spend a minimum of energy in understanding the broadest possible range of things. You are a natural strategic planner but not necessarily particularly tactical. For you to figure out where you need to be in the long haul is both fun and stimulating, but knowing how to play your cards in the short haul can be both frustrating and difficult for you, as the skills required to do that are more situationally oriented than stringing together issues with a strategic impact.

You may be a loner in that you have learned that you cannot expect an equal intellectual contribution from your co-workers. Yet without them, accomplishing the day-to-day tasks might not be possible. You are serious; you believe that "heaven can wait."

The Idealist

Your genius as an entrepreneur is in bringing people together and working harmoniously with them, both within your organization and with suppliers, clients, and customers. The fact that you are or aspire to be an entrepreneur is likely to be motivated by forces quite different from the forces that move individuals who want to beat the world, make money, and leap tall buildings, so to speak. Your prime interest in life, above and beyond all material wealth, is people. You are fascinated and energized by them, and have an innate love for fellow human beings.

As an entrepreneur, you are likely to fulfill the role of a mentor, and you have the ability to assist and enjoy people both in their personal and professional growth. You also have patience and know that things cannot always happen as fast as you might want them to. In your work, you strive for people to realize their full potential, yourself included. Not surprisingly, therefore, you have a deep sense of integrity and respect for humankind. Although you are a great team player, you may not necessarily be the greatest organizational role performer. Indeed, your team spirit is directed toward people rather than systems and procedures.

You always search for ways people can work together harmoniously, and when things do not go your way you probably procrastinate in confronting people. Indeed, taking that kind of action may be your last resort, and when you do act, contrary to your mild-mannered attitude, you can lash out at people with vehemence. Your anger may not be directed at the individual as much as at the hurt and disappointment you feel when your ideal doesn't work. Of all the entrepreneurs, you have the greatest capacity to dream great dreams, and you embrace the notion that nothing happens until someone has a dream. Sometimes you may confuse your dreams with reality, though, and there are times when you need to be more concrete than abstract in your deliberations. You like to flirt with all the good things in life, and you are a wonderful romantic.

As a result of your intense people-focus, there are times when you can be exploited. Your instincts are usually to believe that things will work out for the common good. Put another way, there may be times when your näiveté gets the better of you.

Finally, as an entrepreneur you will always encounter great success in situations where succeeding is dependent upon people coming together and delivering the best performance they possibly can. The reason is simple: You have great facility with the interpersonal process and you can mastermind circumstances so that people willingly support you and what you want to achieve because they trust your integrity and authenticity.

Now that you know which entrepreneurial style is dominant for you, how you consistently function should begin to reveal itself in myriad of previously unconsidered ways. This knowledge about yourself and others will provide you with great powers of awareness for understanding your path to entrepreneurial success.

CHAPTER TWO

THE FOUR ENTREPRENEURIAL STYLES

Only those who risk going too
far can possibly find out
how far one can go.
—T. S. Eliot

B efore exploring these specific entrepreneurial traits further, it is useful to recognize eight truths gleaned from years of experience, research, and consulting with individuals who successfully ventured outside conventional frameworks to achieve their personal goals and objectives. Implicitly and/or explicitly, entrepreneurs are aware of the following "rules of the road" as shown on the chart on the next page.

With these truths in mind, let us explore in depth how each one of these four entrepreneurial temperaments functions in everyday work-life situations.

Assuming you are comfortable with the description of your own brand of entrepreneurial temperament as outlined in chapter 1, I will now describe in some detail the characteristics of each one of the four in terms of

▲ Orienting yourself

▲ Delivering superior performance

▲ Taking charge of your destiny

▲ Working under uncertainty

Rules of the Road for Entrepreneurs

1. Whether you were born with limited or exceptional capacity to be an entrepreneur, you still have to work relentlessly to produce something of value. Furthermore, no one has consistently been able to deliver superior performance in areas in which they are not gifted.

2. Passionate involvement is essential to fulfill your destiny. Entrepreneurs stretch their imagination while perpetually honing their skills in the face of the reality of today's uncertainties and unpredictable changes.

3. Half measures are out of the question for entrepreneurs who live at the cutting edge. The local, the provincial, the tried and true are fast becoming obsolete in an increasingly global economy.

4. An effective entrepreneur learns to identify and ignore dysfunctional aspects of a work culture and does not live where the group or "collective" live. In the final analysis, the highest challenges are self-imposed. There are no shortcuts for those who arrive at the future first.

5. An entrepreneur worthy of that distinction engages in constructive activities, evolutionary dynamics, and is an asset to the community.

6. The harder you work, the more energy you generate. Although it may appear effortless to an onlooker, skilled and intrepid entrepreneurs have spent years with success and failure, both contributing to their present-day capacity and momentum.

7. Successful entrepreneurs have a knack for identifying essential priorities, while passing over time-consuming trivia.

8. Entrepreneurs are both born *and* made.

▲ Arriving at the future first

▲ Being a member of a community

▲ Determining essentials and priorities

▲ Realizing some entrepreneurs are born, others made

As you familiarize yourself with each one of these four categories, you will begin to understand how each style tends to function and to recognize differences and similarities in your own work-life situation.

The Characteristics of the Administrator

Orienting Yourself

If there is anything the Administrator entrepreneur knows how to accomplish better than most, it is to set up a set of circumstances to get things done in an orderly manner, predictably, accurately, and on time! This type of entrepreneurship is carried out with a deep sense of commitment to duty, honor, and tangible achievements. The Administrator is driven by the need and ability to deal with concrete tasks to accomplish what needs to be done according to predetermined goals and objectives. Seldom, if ever, would an Administrator operate out of impulse and on the spur of the moment. This entrepreneur requires carefully crafted plans, work procedures, and job descriptions with nothing left to chance or speculation. That is why this kind of entrepreneurship is rooted in working with what is known. The Administrator makes his or her best contribution when what needs to be done is explicitly and specifically articulated and understood by everyone involved. In short, these entrepreneurs are at their best in situations where everyone knows what needs to be done in the near future. They are not comfortable with conceptualizing or contemplating what needs to be achieved over the long haul as the circumstances of their enterprise change. They enjoy leading their team to great achievements by ensuring that people are provided with the tools to do the job.

The Administrator assumes his or her entrepreneurial station with little fanfare and flair; rather, he or she keeps in close touch with the day-to-day realities of the organization. Administrators assume the role of entrepreneurship to the point of social responsibility: They enjoy joining both professional and social associations because of their ongoing need to belong to constructive and supportive organizations. Moreover, they are calculated risktakers; if they could have their way, they would carefully manage the resources of the organization, allowing it to continuously deliver competitive goods and services within known technologies and traditional practices. Hence, Administrator entrepreneurs provide a great deal of stability in their leadership pattern and find comfort in established ways of conducting business.

For an Administrator entrepreneur, a potential problem is the danger of getting stuck in established ways of doing things and resisting change. Administrators are in danger of having a false sense of comfort based on familiarity and the security of routine. Another trademark of the Administrator is a need for painstaking control and for fair and equal treatment of people throughout the organization. This entrepreneur puts a premium on loyalty—to the organization and to the people in it. Not surprisingly, therefore, people who are out of line or in violation of regulations are likely to be reprimanded. Seeking security, an Administrator tends to be highly aware of the need to conserve resources and is at all times concerned that the organization remain an efficient vehicle in meeting its obligations and achieving predetermined goals and objectives.

Driven more by obligation and a sense of responsibility to be respected and noted leaders in their community than by any other motivation, Administrators need and enjoy formal associations and recognition for their contribution. They are loyal team members and thrive on maintaining and improving on tradition. These entrepreneurs fear poverty and the absence of essential resources necessary to become high achievers and to live the good life. The Administrator respects factors that perpetuate stability, growth, and a sense of communal purpose in work situations. Therefore, expect Administrators to manifest their significance and importance through ceremonial activities for society to honor and admire.

Delivering Superior Performance

Administrators welcome responsibility and accountability, and they seek to understand the economic aspects of their enterprise. Highly industrious, they have a great deal of respect and concern for the proper employment of scarce resources, energy, money, and time. They enjoy work situations where they can experience predictable and orderly progress. Because they place high expectations and a great deal of pressure upon themselves, it is important for them that everyone else live up to their assigned responsibilities and carry their fair share of the load. In any work situation, Administrators take on responsibility for the continued and appropriate performance of the organization. They are likely to concern themselves with policies, systems, routines, and productivity rather than theories, abstractions, and conceptual models.

Administrators value highly a dependable, loyal, and industrious team. They enjoy being "the salt of the earth," and a verbal promise from these entrepreneurs is as important and valid as any written document. It follows, therefore, that to an Administrator, a broken promise is a mortal wound that can never really heal.

Taking Charge of Your Destiny

Administrators are action oriented. Do not expect these entrepreneurs to be brilliant strategic planners; they prefer to deal with the short-term realities of a given situation. As long as their environment is reasonably predictable and competitive and change happens incrementally, they are likely to do just fine. Hence, they can easily be in charge of their destiny if external circumstances allow them to continue to do what they know well. Be aware, however, that abrupt changes, the introduction of new technologies, and rapid obsolescence can turn an Administrator-led organization to experience turmoil and declining performance. Because similar types of leaders flock together like "birds of a feather," watch out for organizations led by Administrators; they are often unaware of the opportunities to take advantage of people who are more conceptual than they are and who can increase the awareness of the necessity for change and thereby bring new dimensions into the firm. Indeed, Administrators can be so dedicated to what they know that their various departments and organizational units may increasingly interfere with the success of the total firm. In other words, if everyone is doing their duty, the whole system may be in trouble.

Due to their keen economic awareness, Administrators know they need to save for a rainy day. Being careful, calculated risktakers, they are seldom mortally wounded if they have reaped the benefit of success over the years. Hence, they have every opportunity to be in charge of their own destiny as long as there is a keen awareness of the risk of obsolescence and a need for perpetual change.

Working Under Uncertainty

Over time, achievements, increased recognition, and heightened exposure can cause Administrators to gain a premature sense of aristocracy and enjoyment of the respect earned from their contributions to the community. They are, however, inherent team players and therefore are not likely to attempt to shine alone.

Not surprisingly, individuals who appear to be hip shooters and able to thrive in crisis situations are threatening to the Administrator type of entrepreneur. People who are incapable of being responsible on a day-to-day basis and who periodically present ill-conceived ideas may soon find themselves on the way out. Anyone throwing a wrench into the system could be severely punished, to the point of being asked to leave the organization. Uncertainty for Administrator entrepreneurs, in the long run, is not acceptable. An Administrator-type organization is based upon orderly progression, trust, and predictability, and it is important for the Administrator that things are done right the first time. Mistakes—especially if they are repeated—are intolerable. A well-functioning Administrator-type organization ensures that deviations from predetermined standards are, at a minimum, met with mixed feelings and concern for failure. Hence, expect Administrators to always be at their very best when all the pieces fit together, and products or services are delivered on time according to plans and budgets.

Arriving at the Future First

Long-term planning for Administrators does not occur naturally; rather they meet the realistic and specific circumstances of a given situation. Therefore, they are not likely to support brainstorming ideas and deviations from the familiar. These entrepreneurs often use the budget as a tool for measuring success, which, during periods of rapid change, can be extremely dangerous. Expect Administrators to shy away from words and phrases such as *jumpstart, inspiring, great idea, just do it, ingenious,* and a general fascination with the unknown. However, particularly in the initial stages of any organization, the demands that propel the entity must be strong. Yet if these demands are not constantly researched, studied, and understood, an Administrator-type organization can quickly lose its franchise and dwindle into nothingness.

Being a Member of a Community

Administrators have a healthy respect for established traditions and constructive, civil human values. But the notion of the territorial imperative to be "of someplace" is more important than merely "coming from somewhere." Whatever contributes to their positive and constructive position in society provides them with an all-important sense of well-being, security, and belonging. That is why family and organizational events such as birthdays, anniversaries, and holidays hold a special meaning for these individuals. Within their respective communities and organizations, they know how to honor loyalty, longevity, and sustainable contributions. That kind of attitude is frequently transferred into the larger society; they take pride in being significant contributors to the well-being of their entire community. It is important to recognize their need for and sense of belonging and providing value beyond mere economics.

Instinctively wanting to guard against danger, Administrators rely upon the community to fend off threats. Therefore, they always seek to be team players and to contribute for the sake of the whole rather than for their own benefit. On the other hand, they enjoy notoriety for their personal contribution and always cherish moments when they are recognized personally for their unique contributions toward a worthy cause.

Determining Essentials and Priorities

I would venture to argue that there isn't an Administrator-type entrepreneur who, somewhere, somehow, doesn't keep a list of things to do. Indeed, it is quite common to see CEOs of the Administrator kind receive an index card from their secretaries upon which their schedule for the following working day has been neatly typed—or, more likely in this day and age, an e-mail message to their computer. Not having priorities is unthinkable, and not to have something to do is synonymous with not being useful. Hence, their day is usually filled with appointments, meetings, and events that place them in the middle of everything while making a contribution. Idle moments for an Administrator can be threatening. Be aware, though, that although the calendar may be full, the conceptual framework within which this kind of entrepreneur functions may be at risk, for in the heat of the battle, these individuals do not spend a great deal of time reflecting upon "what to be."

The concept of time tends to be important for someone who enjoys organizing and administrating. Therefore, to be on time is important, and proper etiquette in this type of work environment is to take time or even make time with an Administrator. They have a healthy respect for the finite minutes and hours of a day, and they are not likely to have time for chit-chat and personal indulgences. That is not to say that they cannot have a good time; rather, they have a natural capacity to distinguish between work and play time.

Realizing Some Entrepreneurs Are Born, Others Made

It would be folly to categorize Administrator entrepreneurs as either "born" or "made." Perhaps a better concept is to suggest that they slide into entrepreneurship. The notion that background determines expectations suggests that there are Administrator entrepreneurs who at an early age determined that they wanted to enter into the entrepreneurial arena, whereas others find themselves in a situation causing them to take the entrepreneurial route. They prefer not to break away from their families and communities; rather, they grow into situations that lead them into their life's working station.

Perhaps a better approach would be to suggest that successful Administrators tend to be leaders first and then entrepreneurs. They are the type of leaders with a determination to be high achievers, and if entrepreneurship naturally falls into their pattern of activities, they will simply go out and "do the entrepreneur thing." Their success stems from instinctively knowing what to do and initially attracting a few people who can help them achieve their objectives. The age factor for Administrator entrepreneurs is an important variable. When they start out, they devote time and energy to the point of being fanatical about achieving their goals. On entering the mid-life and later life stages, however, they may keep up their good work, but they also enjoy reaping the benefits of their lifelong contributions and may therefore risk losing relevance in fast-changing environments.

As David Keirsey and Marilyn Bates write in *Please Understand Me:*

> Caution, carefulness, thoughtfulness, and accuracy of work are valued by the [Administrator], for he is product oriented. An [Administrator] enjoys comments about whatever he produces, especially if these comments recognize how well the product meets the standards set forth. He appreciates being recognized as responsible, loyal, and an industrious person . . . although they will have difficulty showing their pleasure when recognition is given.

The Characteristics of the Tactician

Orienting Yourself

The Tactician entrepreneur cannot sit back and contemplate. He or she is energized by the need for achievement. These entrepreneurs learn inside the process of doing, so to speak. Indeed, they are people who instinctively know what action to take given ever-changing circumstances. For them the goal is the journey itself. Tactician entrepreneurs are highly flexible and can comfortably roll with the punches. These people know instantly what has to be done *now*, not tomorrow or the next day. They are opportunity driven; strategic planning and long-term contemplation just do not fit their style. Not surprisingly, they are the greatest risktakers, who win or lose it all. Tactician entrepreneurs also somehow find time for both work and play. For them, the world is a stage upon which life is to be acted out, and the position they enjoy is—you guessed it—center stage! For Tactician entrepreneurs, the freedom to act and affect the world is critical; without it, they cannot function.

Tacticians may appear more self-aware and self-centered than Administrator entrepreneurs, although that is not necessarily the case; however, Tacticians derive great satisfaction from their ability to make an impact with their very presence. They are more hands-on than philosophical or administrative. By nature, they can never settle down and are always in a searching mode.

Tacticians tend to know what to do under difficult and trying circumstances. The price paid for this gift is that they are less conceptual and strategic than others. By not paying much attention to long-term cycles, Tacticians can be at a disadvantage in the long run as new technologies emerge. Once they have mastered a trade or a business, they are at their best operating within known parameters. Skillful in assuming variations on a theme, they do not particularly enjoy new activities, which may not turn out to be as rewarding as familiar territory.

Usually gifted negotiators, Tacticians are instinctively assuring and prevailing with the best conditions for their side. They are chameleon-like, though: One moment, Tacticians can be charming, and the next moment they can seem defiant and cold. Once viewed as an adversary, you may never return to the good graces of a Tactician. Although economic success may not be a stated goal, Tactician entrepreneurs at times may achieve windfall profits from their enterprises, as they are more capable than others of functioning in confusing and ill-defined areas: They outmaneuver competitors who may be too structured to notice emerging opportunities. On the flip side, Tacticians may bet the store and lose big.

Tactician entrepreneurs are forever searching for opportunities outside of the established order. Moreover, they believe that success does not come from not failing; rather, they do not let failure stop them. They also abhor authority figures and orders, for they need freedom to be brave in responding to tactical opportunities. Indeed, Tactician entrepreneurs are the connoisseurs of life, the virtuosos who have the ability to fine-tune their organizations to respond to the changing nuances in a competitive environment. Their trust in their own ability to grasp the subtle changes of any situation faster than anyone else allows them to negotiate anything. Their interest in organizational hierarchies is practically nonexistent, for they know what is going on outside of the positions created within the organizational boxes. For them, that is where real life is lived. Indeed, they are the greatest disbelievers in casting people into predetermined roles.

Delivering Superior Performance

Tactician entrepreneurs are consummate performers, for they need to make an impact in any situation in which they find themselves. They also tend to be sticklers for perfection. The more introverted Tacticians do not function well if they cannot be hands-on entrepreneurs; they enjoy being in the thick of events and shaping the activities in their own image. Don't be surprised, therefore, if introverted Tacticians find it hard to delegate, for in their minds others can seldom be as creative as they, and hence they cannot let go. The extraverted Tactician entrepreneur, on the other hand, also works with a flair but has a higher capacity to delegate and thus is not always in control. Tactician entrepreneurs at all times must be heavily engaged in what they do. When bored, they lose their "oomph" and their motivation to maintain high levels of energy and produce astounding results. They have a natural capacity to know what to do in a pinch, and they are masterful in handling crisis situations. I have known highly accomplished Tactician entrepreneurs who enjoy creating a small crisis here and there to keep the adrenaline flowing. The superior performance of Tactician entrepreneurs, therefore, is directly tied to producing stunning results and achievements no one else is able to imitate or repeat.

Taking Charge of Your Destiny

Tactician entrepreneurs are not completely in charge of their destiny. They walk, or rather run, through life with a magic wand; whatever they touch usually ends up being an incredible success or a total flop. For them, the notion of destiny reaches too far into the distance. Their horizon tends to be much nearer, as they are action oriented and need to be *doing*. Do not expect typical Tacticians to be great strategic planners; their strength is in knowing what to do and having a unique sensitivity for choosing opportunities. Their search for perfection is endless.

More than any other entrepreneurial type, Tacticians love excitement. They are at their best with anything that requires extraordinary energy and attention, where the outcome is speculative.

Tacticians have an unusual capacity to live and function in a state of suspended animation. They perceive no boundaries or job descriptions, only skills and talents to be developed. For them, the idea of being in charge of one's destiny is lofty, unrealistic, and trite. They know best how to make the most out of life here and now. Saving for a rainy day may occasionally come to mind, but living life every day to the fullest is always the highest priority.

Working Under Uncertainty

If ever anybody was born to function at full capacity under uncertainty, it is the Tactician entrepreneur. In fact, having to function under predictable and certain conditions twenty-four hours a day becomes so boring to Tactician entrepreneurs that they become preoccupied and eventually will venture onto something else. They come fully into their own when nobody knows what to do, and they love to produce astounding results where others fail.

Tacticians seldom prepare for anything; they instinctively know what to do in each situation, given the peculiarities, particulars, and nuances creating a set of unique conditions. That is not to say that they do not prepare; but their preparation, so to speak, is on the fly as they pick up on subtleties faster, better, and more comprehensively than anyone else. There are times when they create stunning results where others were predicting impending disaster, maximizing each moment with grace and aplomb. When uncertain conditions have been rectified, don't expect them to sit around and enjoy the applause; they are long gone, searching for the next set of dire circumstances where they can make their unique contribution.

Arriving at the Future First

Having a relatively low need for planning to arrive at the future first, Tactician entrepreneurs experience life as "being there" all the time. They are not the type to contemplate and anticipate the future; their absorption in the present prevents that. They are not great philosophers. They are at times blind to abrupt changes in technology and practices within their areas of specialization, but they enjoy developing unparalleled expertise in their fields of endeavor and enhance that expertise by searching for variations on themes they know. Although masterful in functioning under uncertainty, they are well anchored in certainty, in their own skills, and in knowing what to do.

As a result, Tactician entrepreneurs tend not to be great strategic planners. As long as they are in the middle of a stream of activities and can sustain that position, they are likely to function quite well. However, to use a metaphor, they may well be able to supercharge a four-stroke engine and reach performance levels heretofore not thought possible, but that is of low consequence at the eve of the introduction of the jet engine. For Tactician entrepreneurs, it is the adventure *during* the moments of the journey that counts. The arrival for them is anticlimactic.

Being a Member of a Community

Tactician entrepreneurs are fiercely independent, and their sense of community is more related to the enjoyment they derive from it than playing the role of concerned citizens. The community within their working environment exists around the Tactician entrepreneurs. They represent the community within themselves: Wherever they happen to be, that's where the community is, and it stretches from the mailroom to the boardroom unencumbered by hierarchies, job descriptions, and rigid policies. Do not expect Tacticians, therefore, to be particularly enamored with organizational charts and job descriptions. For them, the important thing is to get the job done effectively, efficiently, and with great flair.

The community outside of the work environment for Tactician entrepreneurs tends not to be traditional establishments such as the PTA and other goodwill activities. Yet they may enjoy taking on a role in community politics. Moreover, Tactician entrepreneurs are frequently found in artistic arenas, for they are connoisseurs of grace and beauty and appreciate art and rapport with artists. In any community, though, Tactician entrepreneurs are not consummate team players, for they are rugged individualists.

Determining Essentials and Priorities

Usually acutely aware of client and customer needs, Tactician entrepreneurs are obsessed with delivering product and services of the highest quality and standard. That, however, does not necessarily translate into a clear articulation of the end results and the determination of priorities. In fact they have a "just do it" attitude, expecting all to do their jobs but often not bothering to describe what that job is. Hence, you will often find them in conflict between wanting to deliver superior results and finding it difficult to be on time, partly as a result of a lack of organization and partly because, for them, nothing is ever good enough.

Tacticians are all a bit of a masochist; loving to be in the heat of the battle and producing amazing results with minimum awareness for how to set up schedules, systems, and procedures for arriving at the future first. In the mind of Tactician entrepreneurs, everything tends to be a priority, and therefore there are no priorities. So expect the working day of Tactician entrepreneurs to be filled with activities, many unplanned, because they respond well to unanticipated events. This is not to suggest that Tactician entrepreneurs do not honor time and commitments; rather, it explains the dichotomy of individuals who have a need for keeping a finger in every pie, knowing what is going on, and influencing each situation. The important challenge is to master the outcome and to dramatically affect others.

Realizing Some Entrepreneurs Are Born, Others Made

Are Tactician entrepreneurs born or made? This may be an overstatement, but there are few Tactical entrepreneurs who really are made; most are born that way. They can be highly successful independent entrepreneurs, but they usually are miserable intrepreneurs because they are not very manageable. They like to soar unencumbered by routine and trivia. Tactician entrepreneurs, having once experienced the joy of creating and establishing their own firms and entities, never forget the thrill. Failing in their entrepreneurial endeavors is seldom viewed as a disaster; rather, it might be considered a momentary setback. Unfortunately, a setback could last a lifetime. The entrepreneurial spirit within Tacticians may temporarily fizzle out but it cannot completely disappear. They are always alert to the next bend in the road and the new opportunities to arrive on the scene.

More often than not, Tacticians are relentlessly optimistic: The glass is usually half full. That is not to say that they cannot be pessimistic to the point of being sarcastic, especially when they are hurt or under attack; yet they are always searching for new and undiscovered opportunities. In fact, they are fiercely individualistic and unwilling to take no for an answer. Therefore, when they set out as entrepreneurs, they seem to have boundless energy to drive the organization wherever they want it to go, resulting in smashing success or, at times, miserable failure.

David Keirsey and Marilyn Bates in *Please Understand Me* sum this up:

> [Tacticians] appreciate recognition of the clever, facile ways they work. Commendation for the grace and flair of their actions is more important to them than note of how much work was done. The [Tactician] is process-oriented, not product-oriented. If the work entails risks and taking chances, this should be commented on. When the risks pay off, [Tacticians] need companionship in celebrating the results. When they do not, they need support and encouragement, expressions of comfort that this was merely a temporary setback.

The Characteristics of the Strategist

Orienting Yourself

The Strategist entrepreneur is the self-sufficient individual whose entire outlook is the future. "Today" is obsolete, and only "tomorrow and beyond" capture the attention, imagination, and energies of the strategist. He or she is obsessed with "what to be," and the mundane day-to-day stuff holds no promise of grand achievements. This entrepreneur never takes no for an answer and consistently advances the goal line, ensuring a dynamic environment with no real end in sight. The strategist cannot rest on achievements for very long and is forever searching for a better mousetrap and levels of achievement no one else can match.

These intuitive individuals derive great satisfaction from dealing with concepts, ideas, and abstractions. Their level of patience for specific and concrete routinized work can dwindle faster than the best of intentions compared to a concrete day-to-day kind of person. If Strategist types swear on a stack of anything that they are consummate team players, don't believe it. They may play with the team, but when push comes to shove, they are independents whose self-confidence sometimes borders on arrogance.

Strategist entrepreneurs tend to take the high road, deriving more satisfaction from intellectual pursuits than from actual operating challenges. They are fascinated by strategies, and they are at their best when they can add value today to outperform competition tomorrow. For them, it is unnatural not to live in the future. Unlike Tactician entrepreneurs, Strategist entrepreneurs are more concerned with what they can eventually achieve by being insightful and brilliant than they are with taking advantage of a situation on the fly.

Strategists have little time for fools. They tend to see themselves as having an intellectually pleasing sense of humor and being charming and easy to get along with. At times, this perception could not be further from the truth because in everything they do they apply reasoning, logic, and brainpower—but not much else. Strategist entrepreneurs represent the Protestant work ethic well: You will not find them walking in a meadow, smelling the flowers; they would much rather be somewhere else demonstrating their exceptional capability in designing stunning strategies. Strategist entrepreneurs are acutely aware of the value of scarce resources, particularly those tied to economic values. They search for ways to utilize resources as efficiently and as comprehensively as possible. Ultimately, Strategist entrepreneurs are builders for the future rather than day-to-day operators.

These types delay present gratification in anticipation of future success. They are perpetually climbing the next mountain with a limited ability to enjoy the view because in front of them is the next mountain. They will never be champions of daily routine or business as usual; rather, they realize how different forces perpetually change the substance and form of an organization. Moreover, Strategist entrepreneurs strive to replace bureaucracy with meritocracy. They believe that the best person will win, so naturally they do not spend much time establishing warm long-term human relationships, finding them time consuming and not particularly predictable.

Delivering Superior Performance

Strategist entrepreneurs are at their best when allowed to deal with concepts, ideas, and the future; their contribution is one of staking out the course for an organization. Thus, they do not perform very well the day-to-day routine tasks which are necessary to make an organization function. Indeed, they can be both intellectual giants and snobs. They can also talk out of both sides of their mouths at the same time and enjoy an argument for the sake of gaining insights and learning.

Strategist entrepreneurs are usually aware of the need for the team to reach ambitious goals and objectives but are not really a team players. Nevertheless, they will play with the team to achieve astounding results but in the final analysis each remains a loner. Such individuals take great pride in being highly competent and in having exceptional expertise in their own areas of particular interest. On the other hand, if they view something as trivial, menial, and routine, they are indifferent to it. When they are at peak performance, they appear cool, aloof, and distant as they demonstrate their capacity for foresight. Strategist entrepreneurs are at their very best when they don't have to be bothered with today and can arrive at the future long before anyone else suspects it is here. The best contribution of Strategist entrepreneurs is to be involved today with the critical issues required to secure a brilliant tomorrow.

Taking Charge of Your Destiny

Not only do Strategist entrepreneurs want to be in charge of their own destiny, they also tend to take charge of everybody else's. The Introverted Strategist does it by engineering a set of conditions so superior the team wouldn't dream of quitting. The Extraverted Strategist entrepreneur tends to marshal all available resources to charismatically storm the next hill—and thereby elicit loyalty.

Not likely to be of a mind to save for a rainy day, Strategist entrepreneurs are highly dynamic and trust their own ability to create conditions that are so superior that they don't need to bother taking care of their personal finances. They strive to be both effective and efficient; they like to focus their energies on doing the right things, not just doing things right. Hence, they have a very real sense for priorities, directing their energies into areas where the results are likely to be the most beneficial.

The process of being in charge of their destiny involves both the intellectual and visual domain. Evolving a vision and then making it happen provides Strategists with more satisfaction than does financial success alone. They are enamored with the design and the opportunity to resolve complex issues in difficult situations better and faster than anyone. In the final analysis, ideas of how to be in control of their future are more meaningful for them than either dealing with the actual implemention of plans or enjoying the fruits of their hard labor.

Working Under Uncertainty

Highly flexible, Strategist entrepreneurs thrive on operating with insufficient information, while remaining open for new data. They have a high need to guide and marshal people and resources in directions usually carefully thought out, and they are masterful in doing so. But when their organization is not performing as anticipated, they can get quite "uptight" and become preoccupied with issues outside the central core of a problem. And if their path becomes overloaded with uncertainty, they tend to become temporarily immobilized, and they flounder. Mild degrees of uncertainty, however, can energize them into providing better solutions in changing circumstances. Be mindful of the fact that for Strategists, the boredom of day-to-day routine is worse than navigating in uncharted waters. If short-term surprises appear, however, they are not necessarily tactically astute and capable of making the best possible decision. With the aid of time, they can figure out just about anything, but because so much of their focus is on the future, they can be paralyzed by negative events close at hand.

Arriving at the Future First

Strategist entrepreneurs never arrive. They are obsessed with making sense of current events in light of the future. They are at their best when challenged to anticipate the future and at their worst dwelling with the past. They know that their organization is obsolete, as it was designed for past activities and inevitably will become less competitive and relevant. Thus, they are forever asking the kinds of questions that lead to a new understanding of possibilities. Coming up with the right answer to the wrong question for Strategists is retrograde. Therefore, you will find them frequently probing and exploring concepts whose time has not yet come. Once they know that activities have been categorized and put in their proper working perspectives, they quickly lose interest and intellectually move on.

Impatient with the operating side of their business, Strategist entrepreneurs want to become better but not necessarily bigger. Hence, growth is not accomplished by quantity alone: Improving quality may be even more important.

In the end, though, Strategists are prepared to relinquish control to others more capable than themselves so they may continue to pursue their journey into the challenges of the future.

Being a Member of a Community

Being part of a community is not a high priority for Strategists. That is not to suggest that they don't appreciate the communities in both their business and personal lives, but communities are not built by Strategists. They are too individualistic to find satisfaction in community membership. That doesn't mean they do not join, but their joining is more out of obligation than out of need or desire.

In the external environment, too, Strategist entrepreneurs function in whatever community seems appropriate, more as a result of obligation and proper positioning than attempting to be a valuable contributor. Indeed, their heart may not be involved, but their head is. In the internal community of their work situation, they usually take on a commanding position directing people and assisting them in determining what they need to do. They seem to know what is best for others. Frequently, the internal communities within their respective organizations are there to serve the intellectual needs of the Strategist entrepreneur and not the other way around. They only have use for an internal community if it serves the purpose of strengthening the competitive position of their enterprise.

Determining Essentials and Priorities

Strategist entrepreneurs cannot function well without knowing the changing dynamics and essential characteristics of their businesses. Their priorities emanate from an insatiable need to create conditions that allow their respective organizations to sustain success over long periods of time.

In working with their staff, they can be sticklers for details and for following up on goals. This is done more to keep people alert and focused than because of an interest in control and in reporting on routine matters. It is the interpretation and the meaningfulness of day-to-day activities that gives them the impetus to contemplate and anticipate how things change and how to set new priorities.

The sustaining success for Strategists is grounded in searching for and improving their competence in specific fields of endeavor. They are vitally interested in the dynamics and the inconsistencies in complex issues, and their whole sense of priority-setting is based upon the idea of outperforming their competitors. In the final analysis, what is important is to constantly define, redefine, and comprehend the changes in the competitive environment and to construct new parameters for sustained success.

Realizing Some Entrepreneurs Are Born, Others Made

Strategist entrepreneurs are both born and made. Whether they head up their own organizations or find themselves in the employment of others, Strategists, not unlike Tacticians, are at times difficult to work for, as their minds wander across the constraints, routine, and discipline of everyday work life. They tend to be natural leaders as a result of their need for foresight and often take carefully selected people with them on their journey to the future. From an early age, born Strategist entrepreneurs effortlessly seek to differentiate themselves from the crowd. The "made" kind, however, frequently find that life in a larger organization is neither acceptable nor compatible with their needs; therefore, they begin to prepare themselves under the umbrella of their current job to eventually venture out on their own. If they are allowed to practice their entrepreneurship within an existing organization, they can be valuable contributors where there is potential for growth and new developments. Like the Tactician entrepreneurs, Strategists are highly independent and therefore do not naturally fit into environments calling for conformity. These individuals honor diversity and individuality and remain entrepreneurs all their lives.

As Keirsey and Bates write in *Please Understand Me:*

[Strategists] want to be appreciated for their ideas. They want an intelligent listener who will take the trouble to follow the complexities of the [Strategist's] conception. Seldom does a [Strategist] enjoy comments of a personal nature; rather, he responds to recognition of his capabilities. Appreciation by management of a routine task well done would not only not delight a [Strategist], but might even make him suspicious of the manager.

The Characteristics of the Idealist

Orienting Yourself

Idealists have an enduring, authentic, and compassionate love for people. Not the everyday taskmasters, they inspire people to perform at their very best. Don't mistake this type for a pushover, though. To the contrary, Idealists can be tough as nails in meeting deadlines and accomplishing what needs to be done—without the use of force or pulling rank. Idealist entrepreneurs believe that somewhere in the future a dream will become a reality and all will be well; people will gather and celebrate their achievements and show appreciation for one another in the tasks accomplished. Idealists are easily bruised and takes criticism personally. Part of the reason for this is that the Idealists' investment in people and their ability to achieve great things through teamwork is so great that failure is not an acceptable alternative. Idealist entrepreneurs are the consummate dreamers, almost believing that imagination is reality.

Distinguished by a holistic sense of being, Idealist entrepreneurs tend to be devoted to a cause, to an idea, and to people. Their rewards come from giving to co-workers, clients, and customers. They enjoy being personable and making people feel special. They shy away from confrontation and conflict and want people to feel like members of one happy family. Their happiness comes from harmonious interrelationships and always striving to serve. Indeed, Idealist entrepreneurs tend to be so idealistic that they sometimes deprive themselves of taking advantage of short-term economic benefits.

In addition to the financial element, the major investment of Idealists is in people. They are skillful in listening more to what people intend to communicate than what they actually say, and they have an unusual capacity for being lovable, caring, and accommodating. They are particularly gifted in bringing people along developmentally, eventually maximizing their performance potential. Idealist entrepreneurs tend to be kind and warm and at times are very persuasive. Consider the Idealists to be driven more by values than by analysis. Those values are a behavioral expression of integrity, commitment, and an ingrained desire to make every situation reach its full potential.

These people dream great dreams and build the most spectacular castles in the air. At times, it is difficult for them to accept that the dream is not reality. Henry David Thoreau said, "If you have built castles in the air, your work need not be lost; that is where they should be. Now put the foundations under them." Idealists need to put foundations underneath their castles; they need to realize that to achieve "what to be," they need the support of people who know "what to do." Unlike their counterparts, Idealist entrepreneurs believe that they need to create an environment that allows people to be the very best they possibly can be. Indeed, they believe that policies and procedures do not reform people or make them productive, nor do objective demands and instilling a sense of corporate duty. Instead, Idealists allow people to dispense with as many formalities and rituals as possible. Idealists want them to apply their skills, expertise, and resourcefulness, concentrate on substance, and thus find meaning and happiness.

Delivering Superior Performance

Idealist entrepreneurs are uniquely gifted in creating harmonious conditions where people come together to perform well. Although they can work within traditional organizational parameters if it is expected, they do not believe in impersonal hierarchies, structures, and procedures; rather, they rely on inspiration. Furthermore, they will circumvent and climb over restrictions and artificial rules to reach their goals. The superior performance delivered by Idealist entrepreneurs originates in building strong people organizations by minimizing politics and by replacing hard-knuckled competitiveness with personal commitment and deep human caring. However, Idealists can be fiercely competitive and enjoy winning, as long as mutually supportive relationships are not tarnished and everyone adheres to the same ethical guidelines. Not surprisingly, they find their deepest sense of satisfaction when they step back and see that everything works and people hardly knew they were there.

Taking Charge of Your Destiny

Again, unlike the other entrepreneurial styles, a concept such as "being in charge of your destiny" doesn't really fit Idealist entrepreneurs because the concept is too earthbound; they believe a higher and more spiritual order outside of their control is in charge of their destiny. Frequently, you will find Idealist entrepreneurs seeking counsel from mentors who can bring their organization into a holistic, harmonious whole. Material wealth may be less important than inner peace and harmony because an internal harmonious state is something money cannot buy.

Idealist entrepreneurs have tremendous affection for the people they relate to and work with on a day-to-day basis, including those beyond the boundaries of their organizations; they trust their personal relationships to provide goodwill throughout their working lives. In fact, Idealists appear to be so concerned about others that they may be more involved in helping others to reach their destinies than in finding their own. But if they experience discord, distrust, and conflict, their devotion can turn to dislike. Thus, the destiny of Idealist entrepreneurs is tied inextricably to people and to the environments where they work.

Working Under Uncertainty

Although Idealists derive satisfaction and positive energy from pleasant relationships, in providing leadership for their enterprise they are nevertheless highly capable problem solvers and can deal with uncertainty quite well. Indeed, when making decisions under situations of uncertainty, their intuition can be critical for success. They seem to have a sixth sense for knowing when to take action. Says Nick Watry, one of our Idealist entrepreneur contributors, "For me, timing is everything. We would never have experienced the success we have enjoyed if I had buckled under when pressured to make critical decisions with less than half the information necessary." When under pressure and working with uncertainty, however, Idealists thrive on positive feedback and support from the people with whom they work. They like to be admired; better yet, they love to be loved and will take giant steps in response to modest positive feedback. The ability to work in uncertain circumstances can actually turn out to be a great strength for Idealists in a supportive environment, a stimulating challenge that allows them to explore new ways to effect productive change. This is not to suggest that they thrive on uncertain conditions; on the contrary, they are at their best when the rules of the game are known and when they are allowed to bring to bear the best human resourcefulness they possibly can.

On the other hand, the kind of uncertainty that is loaded with negative sentiments is, for Idealists, an entirely different matter. They intensely dislike confronting people, so if the uncertainty stems from conflict, distortion of information, or withheld knowledge, Idealists are not likely to take it lightly. Left out of the loop, expect Idealist leaders to sulk and feel sorry for themselves. In remedying this kind of uncertainty, they are likely initially to make every effort to re-create predictability and mutually supportive relationships to adequately cope with the lack of information and knowledge. If, for whatever reasons, the Idealist entrepreneurs are incapable of gaining the support needed, watch out, for an Idealist can lash out with a passion and sophistication that leaves others virtually speechless. These outbursts do not happen often, and the ones regretting the confrontation the most are probably the Idealists themselves.

Arriving at the Future First

Idealist entrepreneurs are value driven; although being on the leading edge is important for them, it is vital that the cost of success does not jeopardize the ongoing quality of constructive human relationships. Hence, the very process of approaching the future is more important than arriving. If getting there is experienced as harsh, impersonal, threatening, and cold, Idealist entrepreneurs would rather stay where they are and, if need be, go down with the ship. However, they are relentlessly looking for solutions, and more often than not they evolve an inspirational vision of what the future can be—with plenty of followers. However, if the price for getting there involves a great deal of conflict, they will choose not to embark upon or continue that journey.

In preparing the organization to move forward, Idealist entrepreneurs strive for their key people to grow and develop both personally and professionally in sync with the growth of their organization. They are immensely loyal to those who apply themselves and do their very best. If they suspect someone of having a hidden agenda, that worker is not likely to be invited to participate in the continued growth and development of the enterprise.

Idealists can dream themselves into the future better than any other entrepreneurial type. Getting there, however, can be an entirely different matter. If people do not thrive and support one another, Idealist entrepreneurs create a holding pattern and replace whatever ambitions they had for future success with down-to-earth concern for creating or re-creating conditions for mutual support, inspiration, and harmony.

Being a Member of a Community

Because Idealist entrepreneurs are both highly community focused and builders of human relationships, the premise upon which they would enter any community, either within their own organization or society at large, is predicated upon people respecting one another and being mutually supportive and civil in their actions. Hence, they join communities with the intent of tapping into human resourcefulness, building sound foundations, and allowing members to be or to become whatever they are capable of. Any time Idealist entrepreneurs discover discord and political jockeying for space, they quickly become disenchanted, and they eventually distance themselves both from individuals and from organizations that do not adhere to constructive and supportive ethics.

Idealist entrepreneurs enjoy assuming leadership in situations where there is a momentum and an inspiration to reach goals and objectives of high quality and standards. Nevertheless, they do get hurt more easily than other entrepreneurs, and may abandon their leadership position if they do not feel unique, appreciated, and special to the people they serve.

Determining Essentials and Priorities

The priorities determined by Idealist entrepreneurs are strongly related to their needs for achieving important goals and high aspirations through and with people. Hence, their priorities are shaped by the importance of relationships. Typically, they have clear visions of what they want to achieve; they also intuitively know how to get where they want to be.

They are not likely to mechanically produce a "to do" list. Rather, they carefully review how they can optimize their performance, given the chemistry within and outside their respective organizations. More often than not, a bond emerges between Idealists and the people they rely upon for producing superior results.

Although Idealists can be highly results-driven, they find it exceedingly difficult to perform within a rigid system, because they need to factor in how they will work with people to produce both effective and efficient results. There are no priorities too large or too small when it comes to making a contribution in the lives of other people—to the point of being totally absorbed and fascinated by the challenge of inspiring others. Hence, the priorities of an Idealist may be viewed as mastering the art of motivation; this focus is more important than enforcing a job description or creating a prescribed "to do" list. In the final analysis, the Idealist entrepreneur strives to create a climate in which people are challenged to be responsible and to enjoy their freedom in taking positive action.

Realizing Some Entrepreneurs Are Born, Others Made

Idealist entrepreneurs may be born into situations where they take over as the second or third generation of leadership for an ongoing business. More often than not, however, those who become this style of entrepreneur seem to slide into the role by circumstances neither designed nor thought of as an entree into entrepreneurship. In other words, Idealists frequently happen to be at the right place at the right time and are involved in activities that lead them to assume leadership in up-and-coming organizations. They tend to grow quickly into positions where they discover their capabilities to assume an unusual kind of leadership, whereby through and with people, they begin to produce outstanding results. They may not be born entrepreneurs, but when they are at the point of assuming leadership, they realize that they have an inborn capacity to understand how their organization can deliver superior performance. In other words, they are natural leaders and entrepreneurs. The trick is to find themselves in an evolving situation where their skills and talents are utilized and valued.

Whether Idealist entrepreneurs happen to be born or made, they attach themselves to their organizations and their people with so much strength and dedication that it is virtually impossible for them to want to depart and/or give up their position, especially if an environment has been created where everyone is encouraged and allowed to "do their own thing."

As Keirsey and Bates write,

[Idealist types] want to be recognized as unique persons making unique contributions, and they need an awareness of this stated by their subordinates, peers, and superiors. The other three styles can handle negative criticism more easily than can the [Idealist types], who become immobilized and discouraged when met with negatives. It is important to an [Idealist type] that his feelings as well as his ideas are understood by others and he wants constant feedback concerning both as verification.

CHAPTER THREE

THE ADMINISTRATOR

Becoming number one is easier
than staying number one.
—Bill Bradley

We expect Administrator entrepreneurs to be persistent, stable, responsible, and devoted to the job. Administrators are highly control oriented, focused on establishing the rules of the organization and a predictable, although not necessarily imaginative, working environment. These leaders make up their minds in a methodical, logical, and linear fashion; they do not operate impulsively.

It is reasonable to assume, too, that Administrators are tenacious and personally involved in as many aspects of the organization as possible. The introverted Administrators at times get bogged down in details of micromanagement, their need for perfection preventing them from seeing the big picture. On the other hand, the extraverted Administrators are more likely to delegate and exercise administrative skills by working through and with people, although they do not always pay enough attention to important details.

Sincere, no-nonsense, and hands-on Administrators tend to demand as much of others as they do of themselves. Therefore, if people do not perform up to the high expectations of these leaders, the overall organizational climate will suffer and may eventually become uncertain and conflictual, resulting in declining performance.

Some Administrator entrepreneurs fall into their specific work situations through circumstances that they neither control nor seek to understand. Indeed, often these entrepreneurs happen to be at the right place at the right time. Unlike other entrepreneurial types, they have such a high need for continuity in their work that they're not likely to divert their attention to opportunities outside the mainstream of their tried and true endeavors; rather, they are likely to stick to the job throughout their working lives. They're also likely to hone their skills and consistently seek perfection within their familiar and well-known work discipline.

Initially, Administrator entrepreneurs may appear hard, cold, and calculating. Yet people who get to know them over time will find that they care deeply for individuals to whom they are committed. The manifestation of their concern for people, however, is revealed more by their deeds and actions than by what they say. Indeed, you may find Administrator entrepreneurs short on sensitivity but long on establishing lifelong, productive, satisfying, and predictable working relationships.

Often, Administrators are seen as "nose to the grindstone" individuals, boring and lacking in imagination, careful, pragmatic, and suspicious of anything "not invented here." But when they have a concrete image of what they want to achieve, they can become excited and committed. It is useful to think about Administrator entrepreneurs as people who are most comfortable when allowed to develop all the expertise they can muster in a specific direction. Not "dreamers and schemers," they are at their best when business is carried out predictably, in an orderly fashion, and in accordance with traditional and proven practices.

The performance of Administrator leaders may decline when internal problems demand attention and energy, causing the Administrators to neglect changing external realities. In other words, such leaders become so absorbed within the organization that they lose touch with the changing dynamics in the marketplace and become frustrated when reminded of the need to retool. Administrator entrepreneurs wants a concise and unambiguous definition of "what to do," not necessarily "where to go." Thus, when their need for operational certainty overrides the organization's need for renewal, the Administrator organization enters the danger zone.

Indeed, there are times when these entrepreneurs become so absorbed with traditional activities and a sense of duty toward what they know that they lose touch with the conceptual base that made them successful in the first place.

Finally, Administrator entrepreneurs enjoy their success by the recognition they receive both from within their working environment and from the external environment they serve. Their offices are often filled with memorabilia from past achievements, such as diplomas, framed letters, and autographed pictures depicting them shaking hands with the rich and famous. They also seek membership in clubs, service organizations, and societies with a significant profile both within their work discipline and in the community at large. Typically, these entrepreneurs are joiners, donating time, financial support, and effort to worthy organizations established to improve their community as well as the quality of life for its members.

Role

In addition to delivering quality work and services and adding more value than their critical competitors, at times it is easier for Administrator entrepreneurs to fall into a role of managing as opposed to providing leadership. There may be a temporary loss of vision propelled by their need to resolve unforeseen crises and short-term problematic situations. Hence, they are well advised to both intellectually understand and emotionally accept that in the final analysis their primary role is to be aware of the ongoing need to move their organization into the future.

It is natural for Administrator entrepreneurs to assume responsibility for the quality of their work products and to ensure that the organization performs in accordance with their expectations. As a result it is not uncommon for these leaders to experience stress, which causes them to become both insensitive and authoritative. When successful concepts begin to wear thin, margins begin to reduce, and performance declines, Administrators begin to fill the conceptual vacuum with the wrong remedies: unreasonable demands, excessive use of power, and indiscriminate application of authority. Hence, they are well advised to realize that to sustain success frequently requires an ability to anticipate change by using imagination, flexibility, and skills in coping with the unknown—all areas that neither fit nor particularly excite the highly structured Administrators. On the contrary, these entrepreneurs are more productive and satisfied in conditions where innovations and changes in demand occur in slow, long cycles while business is performed as usual. The natural, and best contribution for Administrators, therefore, is one in which impulsive changes and surprise technologies take a back seat to predictability and routine operations.

Modus Operandi

Administrators are involved in action-oriented activities. Typically, their working day is filled with meetings of groups and individuals to monitor and improve products and service. If standards for performance are not met, some of these leaders are inclined to punish rather than remedy a deteriorating situation; to find fault instead of looking for the reasons behind the problem; to become upset instead of understanding; to become authoritative instead of searching for solutions; and to become bogged down in a microperspective rather than an all-inclusive process. Conversely, when the well-functioning Administrator entrepreneurs are at peak performance, there are no unexpected negative events or surprises.

It is easy for Administrator entrepreneurs to fall into the trap of being concerned about efficiency, "doing things right," rather than being effective, "doing the right things"; usually it is more important for them "to do" than "to be." They tend to be linear and hierarchical in their thinking; for them, there is cause and effect. For example, when something happens, Administrators think it can be traced back to a specific event; they don't see the often complex and multilevel dynamics in a conflict situation. To deal with a multiplicity of processes can, for them, be both difficult and irritating, preventing them from comprehending the total scope of a given set of circumstances. As a result of this limited perspective, Administrators are inclined to believe that simple solutions can be found to complex situations, which is seldom the case. Therefore, it is not uncommon for these entrepreneurs to be fatalistic: When they lose control of situations, they worry, knowing they are neither capable of nor inclined to find new, permanent solutions.

Values

Administrator entrepreneurs prefer the concrete to the abstract and cooperation over individuality, seeking conformity rather than valuing differences. Thus, their organizations may stagnate: Sustainable growth is more likely to come from honoring differences among people rather than enforcing conformity.

Because these entrepreneurs place value on stability and predictability, they are not opportunists who jump on the first available bandwagon. Although Administrator leaders do not shy away from taking risks, they like to know their odds. They tend to approach uncharted territory with the best possible assumption base, a map, and a good compass—not just a compass.

As mentioned, Administrator entrepreneurs, being naturally conservative, want to be concerned: They feel obligated to provide for their people. They also tend to put a premium on manifestations of achievement by initiating and institutionalizing pomp and circumstance. Moreover, those Administrators who have a bent in the direction of the Tactician may tend to assign slightly more value to the "pomp" than to the "circumstance."

Beyond the work situation, Administrator entrepreneurs care deeply for those with whom they are bonded through blood lines and friendship and, they celebrate birthdays, anniversaries, and holidays. They place a high priority on being a team player. Consequently, those co-workers deviating from whatever norms are set by these entrepreneurs may eventually find themselves on the sidelines.

Expectations

Perhaps the single most recurring belief among all Administrator entrepreneurs is the belief in "doing one's duty." For them, performing within an organizational structure is an impersonal affair, removed from the vagaries of personal emotions. Anyone working in a predominantly Administrator entrepreneurial environment who attempts to manipulate or escape his or her responsibility to people and the organization is likely to be judged decisively and harshly. Administrators view their word as their bond, and can neither understand nor accept individuals who tend to shift in their commitments. There are few if any acceptable excuses for not delivering according to plan. Because they expect people to be unbendingly loyal to each other, and, because they expect the organization to provide them with meaningful work and a livelihood, Administrators also expect people to arrive early, work through lunch, and stay late.

Administrator entrepreneurs tend to be obsessed with establishing norms and standards of performance. Although they frequently demand more of themselves than others, the performance expectations they place on people less capable than themselves may at times turn out to be unreasonable, unobtainable, and impractical. There are also times when Administrator entrepreneurs simply refuse to be flexible and take into account impending and inevitable change. In short, the expectations of Administrator entrepreneurs can be somewhat taxing on those with differing values and personal agendas.

Finally, Administrator entrepreneurs tend to assume that once a direction has been set and goals and objectives determined, everyone involved will take heed and accomplish their tasks. Don't be surprised if these entrepreneurs secretly want people to produce admirable results in just about half the normal time. They expect people to be excited and motivated, always striving to deliver superior performance. When these organizational expectations are not met, Administrators frequently confront those employees and demand improvement or force them to live with the consequences.

Lifestyle

Administrator entrepreneurs are hard workers, although not necessarily intellectually superior. They may spend endless hours at work to achieve ambitious goals and objectives, but they are also fulfilling their own sense of purpose and their need to make a contribution. Therefore, expect them to be devoted to their next of kin, their friends, and their families. Indeed, one might suggest that Administrators typically work hard and play hard.

Administrator entrepreneurs, because they like predictable routines, divide their everyday work life into specific task-oriented segments, such as starting the day in a predetermined fashion, be it opening the e- or regular mail, or having a staff meeting to get the day underway. An Administrator we have worked with for years is jokingly called the "fifteen-minute Lloyd"—Lloyd's day consists of forty fifteen-minute segments.

Administrator entrepreneurs are natural competitors who enjoy competing as team members rather than as individuals. They believe that peak performance occurs when teams of people are so committed to and energized by delivering the best possible results that it no longer matters which individual gets the credit.

Although they tend to worry about their work situations and their organizations, it is not unusual for Administrators to leave the work day behind when they finally depart from their office and replenish their energies in non-business-related activities. That, however, does not negate the twelve-hour working days, at times including weekends.

Administrator entrepreneurs have a great capacity for routinizing their working days in order not to miss anything of importance from an operational point of view, but there are times when routines become counterproductive. Even though there is no guaranteed security in managing and operating within previously designed systems and procedures, it may be difficult for highly organized, focused, and loyal Administrators to be mindful of the fact that the long-term security of an organization resides in satisfied and loyal customers.

Let me now introduce you to two Administrator entrepreneurs: Robert Lowe, one of the most successful and highly respected real estate developers in southern California, and Andre Staffelbach, an industrial interior designer who has been honored by every design Hall of Fame for his outstanding work in designing new-age work environments.

▼ Bob Lowe, CEO of Lowe Enterprises

Bob Lowe is the founder and CEO of Lowe Enterprises, a Los Angeles–based real estate firm established in 1972. Over a twenty-four year period, Bob and his team built a diversified real estate company that provides real estate investment, management, and development services to a variety of clients and partners. As an Administrator entrepreneur, Bob has built a formidable organization, currently employing more than 4,000 people and managing over $2.5 billion of assets with over $500 million in annual revenue. He was born in the Midwest and raised in Southern California. He is fifty-six years old and maintains an inconspicuous office in a building on the outskirts of the city.

If there is any one characteristic to define Bob, it is his strong sense of responsibility. That sense of responsibility for just about anything or anyone within his domain is so intense that frequently he does not have enough time to take care of his own needs. As a result of his attitude, there is no turnover among the members of his top team. Bright people are drawn to Bob and enjoy their working relationship with him in a lifelong career.

In reflecting on his formative years, Bob greatly appreciates the values and the lifestyle provided for him by his parents: "My memory of my early childhood is one of a very easy, happy, family-oriented life in which I remember no serious problems and just a lot of love and happiness. I have a hard time remembering negative things. I enjoyed competitive team sports, and I was active in the Boy Scouts. I was also very active in school and served as student body president at every school I attended."

Unlike so many entrepreneurs who strive to break away, Bob made no plans to strike out on his own but eased into his entrepreneurial situation by just being there. His one lifelong commitment, however, is to deliver the best quality work product and provide the best quality service he can. He commented, "I never felt I broke away from the family. At a very young age, I realized the need for a combination of having a great deal of self-respect and family respect along with the willingness to accept responsibility and a great deal of freedom, as long as I was responsible for that freedom. My self-confidence came from my whole life experience. Sure, my success as a student leader contributed to that as well as being a reasonably good high school and a pretty bad college athlete. All those experiences gave me the feedback that I was a fairly good person who had a lot of talent and the ability to accomplish things."

Bob entered into work life well prepared both by the values bestowed upon him by his parents and his strongly developed sense of responsibility and uncompromising work ethic. "The reason I became an entrepreneur was really the result of a series of things that occurred all at the same time. I awoke one day without a job and I didn't have any driving urge to find another job working for someone else. In an informal meeting with my first boss, he suggested, 'Let's form a partnership and I'll put up the money to pay your salary for a year.' So I started this company while I formed a partnership with Victor Palmieri, who was willing to fund enough capital to keep me alive. So we just started. It wasn't as if we started a company without a plan, but I didn't have a plan to start a company."

I asked Bob to reflect on his work in terms of the good, the bad, and the ugly, and he replied, "For me, I need to feel stimulated in what I'm doing. I need to feel as though I am making progress. My ideal work environment is where everybody comes to work and they know what to do. Everybody is excited to work together and accomplish goals we have agreed upon. I have found that when I don't have personal, everyday contact with people, then that just forces more structure into the system. I myself work in a structured way. I mean I have piles for everything that I do and I have lists every day for what I'm going to accomplish. I cross things off, and things I don't cross off I put on my list for tomorrow. We continue to conduct our business, particularly at the more senior level, in a collegial, consensus style where team involvement is encouraged and there is a lot of proselytization amongst various parts of the company. I don't close my door and analyze the situation and then open it and say, 'This is the decision, let's go do it now.' I have everybody participate and I listen, because I am not confident that by myself I can think of all the possibilities. I know, however, if I hear all the possibilities, I can figure out what the right solutions are. So my decision process is inclusive of people because I'm not smart enough to do it myself."

Bob always feels a sense of urgency, sometimes to a point of frustration—even if he is aware that "all the conditions are present for things to be exactly the way they are." The typical Administrator mode for him is problem solving. Hence, the repetitive elements in his working process engender the continuous development of his skills in problem identification and resolution. As a matter of fact, he frequently arranges his working day in such a way that he becomes caught in his own "activities trap." He may not like it, yet he is the master of his own ceremonies.

Bob commented, "I spend much of my time problem solving. I am frustrated by people who aren't dealing with the problem we need to resolve. This wastes time and energy. There are times when I have not been willing to turn things over to other people. It is a function of not having enough confidence to give them total responsibility as opposed to my unwillingness to delegate. The nature of this business is such that every one of us needs to find solutions and get on with it."

By choice, there are issues he is not prepared to delegate to members of his top team, yet Bob is loyal to them. He knows that no one person is smart enough to know all the answers, so his sense of team spirit prevails in everything he does. Indeed, he has attracted people he considers to be smarter than himself and hired them before they were actually needed. Therefore, as new opportunities occur, his company is positioned for action before the competition wakes up to changing circumstances. In reflecting on the performance of two members of his team, Bob assessed the situation as follows: "Brian is successful because he is very smart, very hard working, and a dedicated, loyal person. He doesn't confuse his goals for the company with a lot of other kinds of activities. He has his own management style, and there are times when I can be a good resource for him. John, who has similar characteristics, is also very smart and quick. He is more willing to set goals and delegate. We wouldn't be where we are today if people like Brian and John hadn't been around."

A growing concern in sustaining success in the firm is the issue of succession. Bob and his team have functioned well over the years, weathered storms, matured, and reached levels of performance not thought possible even a few years ago. Transferring their work ethic to the next generation of managers is neither automatically nor easily accomplished, not because the younger members of the management team do not apply themselves or work as hard as their senior colleagues but because the team has not emerged and gelled. Bob explained, "Succession is mainly a competency issue. It is not a matter of distrust. It seems to me the reason you would not delegate something is that you are not sure the person is competent. Or you don't trust them for some reason. I trust people I deal with in this company strongly. One of my primary goals in the next ten years is to build enough strength in the midmanagement level that they will be able to replace our senior team. The driving force in our company is the people who are over forty-five years of age. Yet we have a stated goal of running the company so that it is perpetuated beyond the current generation of top management."

Toward the end of the interview, I asked Bob to summarize what he considered to be the key for Lowe Enterprises to maintain momentum and look to the future with the same kind of enthusiasm and drive that brought the firm to its present stage. He replied, "One of the things my dad always told me was, 'You never start to do anything unless you are going to do it well.' We need for the company always to deliver superior performance, and one of my most important responsibilities is to manage growth. I want to see it done correctly. I'm an overly responsible person—if you can be overly responsible—and that interferes with my willingness and ability to delegate. People almost immediately seem to think I'm a fair, trustworthy person that they would like to be led by, that they could trust. Five years from now, I suspect everything will look very much as it looks today. A succession plan will be in place and I think I ought to make some other changes that I cannot foresee now. I enjoy the notoriety of the success of Lowe Enterprises and the success my wife and I are having in the community. I thoroughly enjoy the time I spend on hobbies, such as learning how to play golf with my friends."

Here we leave a highly successful Administrator entrepreneur who has pursued a career more harmoniously than most. Bob is at peace with himself and his surroundings, both as a result of his established values and his ethical framework, which have allowed him to blend in and lead people with his integrity and deep sense of responsibility. He has a keen knowledge of human temperaments, and in continuing to build his organization he is helping people to reach their potential, given their capability, style, and temperament. Bob will undoubtedly continue to be a gregarious, concrete, logical, systematic, and planful individual who will use his thinking processes and his sense of realism to organize as much of the world as may be his to run.

▼   ## Andre Staffelbach, CEO of Staffelbach Designs & Associates

The entrepreneurial journey of Andre Staffelbach is different, intriguing, and full of unusual events. Andre, age fifty-seven and an interior designer/interior architect, was born in Switzerland and grew up in a frugal, highly controlled environment. Most of what he learned as a child has influenced him throughout his career and made him quite different from the competition.

According to an old saying, "Background determines expectations." Andre's anticipation of what his future would hold was shaped in an environment vastly different from Dallas, Texas, where he currently lives and maintains his office. In reflecting on his upbringing, Andre commented, "We were very poor. I grew up during the years following the second World War, and for us to get by in difficult times, both of my parents had to work. My father was a blue-collar worker and my mother worked as a waitress to help out, so we had some food on the table. We never thought about ourselves as being poor, however, because we always had enough of what we needed. The impression that I still remember, which has haunted me through life and still does, is when my father always said, 'Poor does not have anything to do with cleanliness or taking care of yours and other people's things.' I think that it all boils down into trying to get your employees to be neat. I always tell them it has nothing to do with the salary to have a clean workstation and a clean area to work in."

Andre's office complex, including his own space, has the shape, form, and sanitary look of a living showroom where people go about their work and provide designs known as The Staffelbach Way. His design work is distinct and clearly inspired by his European background.

Until he left Switzerland to come to the United States at age twenty-three, Andre was being prepared for his productive life in a very conservative, old-fashioned way. But he was a highly independent person and did not readily conform to the culture and the strong regimentation of his community. From an early age, he was fascinated by form and fashion and drew whenever he had the opportunity. He explained, "I was always drawing or I was always drafting something. I drew a total spectrum. Whenever I was bored or on a rainy day I would spend hours by myself drawing things. I didn't like my teachers very much. You see, where I went to school the teachers hit or forcefully punished you. When you came home you got another beating because you had upset the teacher."

So by his teens Andre already had one foot in the world outside his hometown. "I always felt that the whole world belonged to me, so therefore it didn't matter where I was or where I ought to be. I knew I would break away early on, and I knew my career would be somewhere else. I really had great problems because from my way of thinking, the Swiss are very controlling and controlled."

Andre did not attend a college or university. Rather, he learned his skills through the traditional apprenticeship process: "When I finished school, which I didn't like too well, I wanted to go into graphic arts, but I was told that there were no apprenticeships available, and the only training I could receive was in interior design, for my parents had no money to send me away to school. So that is what I did." With his diploma in hand, army and employment experience behind him, Andre left for America in 1962. He was able to land work in several cities before he settled in Dallas, where he eventually ventured out on his own. Over the years, his achievements were nothing short of spectacular. Andre has outbid and outperformed larger and more powerful competitors with his smaller, compact, and action-oriented team. Among his trophy achievements are design projects throughout the United States, Europe, and Russia. His clients are many Fortune 500 firms, such as American Airlines, Price Waterhouse, and IBM. Yet even with these high-profile achievements, Andre remains a very down-to-earth person.

"One thing I've learned over the years is that I am my own worst enemy. If it relates to business, I make a lot of dumb decisions. Sometimes with God's help I'm bailed out, and other times I'm not bailed out. I know there are times I need to keep my trap shut—and I don't, and others do not appreciate my style. It's a fine line, and I cannot for the life of me ever accept anything other than the best. I know that sometimes I expect too much of people and that's not fair."

Andre's working philosophies reflect the hardships he encountered and his unrelenting need for perfection. As an Administrator serving clients, he always seeks to surpass himself. He wants to serve his customers better than any competitor, and he does. If and when his people fall down on the job, he "goes ballistic". Those not aspiring to their personal best will find it difficult to work for Andre over the long haul. Indeed, he is a no-nonsense, hands-on leader, having a hard time delegating, as his sense of perfection for the most part resides within himself.

In commenting on his company and his work ethic, Andre said, "All too often people tell me I'm of a different mold, and I don't agree. I was not a particularly good student, and with all the education received by those we hire, I believe they should be quicker, faster, and more perceptive than I am. It is interesting that I seem to have a better understanding and relationship with the craftsmen on the job than the people who want to be important and think they have all the answers. I learned from my father how critical it is to be nice to those people because they are the ones who make everything possible, and they are the individuals who fight harder than anyone else."

His innate respect and caring for his clients is part of Andre's inner makeup and it's impossible for him not to want to meet or exceed their expectations. As he explained, "Once we accept a responsibility, we have to deliver, and we have to live with whatever we have accepted. In other words, if I ask you for something and you say yes, then you do it. There are no 'ifs, buts,' or 'whatevers.' It is simple. People I work well with are flexible because I'm kind of a fireman. I'm all over the place. I work with people from many different angles, and above all I'm very client focused. I know the only reason for us to be here is to keep the client happy and to make things work. It is not our charge to make things more difficult for the clients, which I find many, many people doing."

Andre comes down hard on management. As a result, the turnover of administrative staff is relatively high as incumbents eventually find it difficult to meet Andre's expectations and demands. Andre commented, "Middle management for me is a difficult issue to deal with. It is much less important to think about yourself as a middle manager than to think of yourself as delivering something of value for the client. It is the people on the line who make things happen with managers that lead, not with managers that manage. I know at least twice a year I want to get rid of them because I believe many create more problems than they solve. Managers have too many meetings, too few accomplishments, too much nothing. Some people think I want them to do it my way, and I really don't. I just want the managers to provide us with the best support they possibly can. Many times, I try not to go to their meetings anymore because they take too long. They simply drive me absolutely crazy. Nothing comes from those sessions. I shouldn't say nothing, that's not fair. It is just that too little comes from the management meetings. People don't go into those sessions with 'Wow!'"

Andre experiences a special satisfaction and sense of enjoyment in working with fellow entrepreneurs. In a recent interview with John Scanlon of *The Type Reporter*, Andre said,

> I like working with entrepreneurial CEOs because, good or bad, they have clear ideas. I do not have to sell them ideas, I only have to coax their ideas out. I am the instrument they use. If I walked in and told them, "This is what you need," I'd get a bullet between my eyes. Instead, I put things in front of them so they can shape and choose and in the end be able to say, "I did it."
>
> On other assignments we work with teams from within the company. They are supposed to figure out what is needed, but the problem is that most of these people don't know what they need. They don't understand the organization's business and where it is going as the CEOs do. They don't understand the potential purpose and benefit of the interior design; instead they deal with trivial issues.
>
> I prefer to work with leaders who know who they are and where they are going and what would be best for the future. For example, the CEO of Perot Systems, Mort Myerson, wanted to find a new way for his people to work in the next century. . . . I had to get into his head and understand where the firm was going and he had to open himself up and share his philosophy.

Much like Bob Lowe, Andre is burdened by his sense of responsibility. As an Extraverted Administrator, Bob directs his sense of responsibility to people in his organization. It is interesting to note how Andre is more focused on the responsibility with which he encumbers himself, while serving people and making his own special kind of contribution. He said, "Whatever I do, I'm in it for myself. Not in a selfish way, I just feel that I am responsible for myself. This runs throughout the entire gamut of my life, especially when I get older and have to retire. I don't feel the government owes me anything. I know people say I'm a very successful person, but I have never learned to understand that I'm so successful. That is not what

I set out to achieve. In my mind, I haven't accomplished all that much. I know I'm on a mission, and I guess I don't know the results until the end comes. Then we can determine if it was worth it or not."

Andre, the unwavering, gifted designer, has made a contribution in the work environment for thousands of people. Life for him has been—and for as long as he chooses to work, always will be—riddled with challenges and conflict. The fear of delivering mediocre performance made him an entrepreneur par excellence—never for himself but for those for whom he feels privileged to work. As an Administrator who is close to being a Tactician, Andre never compromises and always pays the price to deliver the best possible work product. Although Andre appreciates compliments, he will remain a humble, hard-working, self-critical, and brilliant entrepreneur.

Over the years of his firm's existence, Andre has received too many awards and prizes to list. It must be said, however, that in addition to holding the national president's title for two organizations, being introduced into the Interior Design Magazine Hall of fame in New York in 1988, and being awarded the Designer of Distinction by the American Society of Interior Designers in 1995, Andre credits much of the success of the business to Jo Heinz, his partner in business and life.

CHAPTER FOUR

THE TACTICIAN

People need a leader to guide
them in the right direction.
    —Beverly Trupp

Under the right set of circumstances, if anyone was born to be an entrepreneur, it would be the Tacticians, who know how to live life with gusto. Tacticians are the born risktakers who find time to smell the roses and replace the everyday humdrum routine with unusual events that make every day unforgettable—provided the conceptual framework of their work has relevance and is in demand. Tacticians can be highly successful: Indeed, they can become striking virtuosos and perfectionists, approaching their work more as an art than a business.

Although usually not hung up on academic and scholarly approaches in their work, Tacticians tend to be such perfectionists that traditional competitors may find themselves handicapped in keeping up. Tacticians are not merely searching for excellence, they provide it uncompromisingly and energetically. There is a distinct sense of freedom in the practice of entrepreneurship for Tacticians because they do not tie themselves down to conventions, theories, and traditional corporate rules and politics. Indeed, they are the ever-present free spirits, directing their energies into areas in dire need of their expertise and creativity.

Unlike other entrepreneurial styles, Tacticians are uniquely capable of enjoying life: They typically play at play and at work too.

Another way of explaining the phenomenon: Tactical entrepreneurs take their work situation—but not necessarily themselves—quite seriously. They seem to find time for everything they like to do. In addition to their entrepreneurship, they are likely to be found trekking in the Himalayas, scuba diving in the Seychelles, helicopter skiing in Canada, conducting an orchestra, being marvelous culinary artists, or, for that matter, coaching the Little League. Tacticians love life for what it is and not for what it could be, because "today" can never be repeated. It is not surprising, therefore, that they are not necessarily motivated to accumulate wealth. They prefer to use the resources within their reach to do what they want in whatever lane they choose, slow or fast.

For other entrepreneurial types, work life may be experienced as constantly shifting tones of gray, whereas Tacticians see it in shades of black and white only, for they go to extremes. They do not shy away from taking risks based more on gut feeling than on careful calculations, and they are challenged by succeeding where others have failed. Also, don't be surprised to find a go-go-go attitude among young, high-energy Tactician entrepreneurs, as opposed to the more seasoned, accomplished senior Tactician entrepreneurs who have a no-no-no orientation, wanting to work less and play more. Indeed, a highly successful fifty-year-old semi-retired real estate developer friend prefers scuba diving in every conceivable body of water in the world to being a workaholic in San Diego.

In an everyday work situation, these entrepreneurs are not bound by convention, tradition, procedures, and job descriptions. They work when and where there is a need, not according to schedules and deadlines, which they neither believed in nor accepted in the first place. One of our interviewees said, "When God created time he created a lot of it. I won't be in the office because I'm supposed to be there. You will, however, find me smack in the center of anything and everything when all hell breaks loose because I know what has to be accomplished when others chicken out, can't cope, or cave in."

Tacticians have the gift of being able to charm the socks off anyone they choose, anytime, anywhere. On the other hand, they can be so caustic, degrading, and demanding that their warmth and kindness can evaporate in a matter of seconds. If, for example, the work product for which they are responsible is below their standards and expectations, they may lash out in anger, disappointment, and frustration.

Introverted Tacticians tend to be more visual than auditory. One of the interviewees said, "I see things through both my eyes and ears," whereas extraverted Tacticians are awakened more by sound than by sight. The auditory types tend to accomplish much of what they want through negotiations. Given these exceptional skills, it would be ill advised to get into a heavy debate or to try to negotiate with them, because they know they are destined to win every time. The visual Tacticians, on the other hand, tend to have highly developed aesthetic gifts along with an unusual ability to see shapes, understand forms, and blend colors.

We experience and expect Tactician entrepreneurs to be the ultimate connoisseurs of life, for they know how to live day by day. At their best on the spur of the moment, they can size up a situation and optimize whatever is there to everyone's benefit. The price they pay for their great Tactician awareness can be found in their less developed side, the Strategic side: Although masterful in taking advantage of the moment, they do not necessarily understand long-term cycles; their gift is knowing "what to do," not "what to be." They have a low tolerance for pontificating and for concepts and underlying theories for why things happen. They *make* things happen, so who cares about philosophies and theories? Perhaps that is one reason why abstract-oriented people find Tacticians so difficult to talk to.

Role

Tacticians are the consummate operators. They derive a great deal, if not all, of their satisfaction from affecting people. They like to know that they are making a difference in any situation with which they are involved.

These entrepreneurs do things with flair. They are pros, spectacular performers, and they achieve amazing results with ease and grace, loving every opportunity to be admired and to demonstrate their great gift of showmanship. Don't expect them to make a contract for life, however. Although their attitude is certainly not one of "easy come, easy go," when they have achieved what they set out to do, they easily get bored and then go searching for the next challenge, detaching themselves from the routines of yesterday. Throughout their working lives, Tactician entrepreneurs may well be involved in a multiplicity of opportunities that are not necessarily strategically tied together. Richard Bronson, the British entrepreneur who started Virgin Atlantic Airlines, is a good example of that. After founding Virgin Records in 1970 (which he sold in 1992 to Thorn EMI) Mr. Bronson went to establish a wide range of successful enterprises—including a cinema chain, a radio station, a soft drinks company, and an exclusive carribean island resort—in addition to the world famous airline.

Tactical entrepreneurs are particularly gifted in making the most of and orchestrating known opportunities, not necessarily being conceptual giants, for the role they master so superbly is to get the most out of whatever is in front of them.

Modus Operandi

Tacticians cannot be aloof and detached. They are typically driven by the need of the moment and associated action. For example, a prominent owner of an automobile dealership realized that the new model cars were not properly displayed in front of the store so as to appeal to bypassing tire kickers and customers. Knowing that no one could rearrange the vehicles as well as he could, he proceeded to single-handedly repark sixty-two cars in less than four hours in front of an admiring crowd of salespeople. Moreover, he claimed that sales increased by 20 percent the following week.

Tacticians have a highly developed sense of aesthetics. What they see, hear, touch, smell, and feel motivates their involvement in such areas as architecture, construction, distribution, the culinary arts, pottery throwing, glass blowing, and similar hands-on operations.

More often than not, these entrepreneurs are optimists, and failing in anything is unthinkable; incurring substantial losses is viewed as a momentary setback for them. They are only defeated when they lose command of their faculties. The modus operandi of the Tactician entrepreneur is inextricably tied to the action: They will, metaphorically, leap tall buildings to achieve what no one else can, and the result of this total involvement is an admirable performance.

Values

Tacticians trust their impulses. Don't expect them to embrace annual retreats and cumbersome strategic plans, for they are opportunity driven, looking for what might be around the next bend. Also, although they want to be progressive, they do not want to be radical. They are experiential learners, striving to be perfect in whatever they do. Having established a successful and trusted pattern, they prefer variations rather than navigating in uncharted waters.

These entrepreneurs value authenticity, and they are exceptionally sensitive to manipulation, fakery, or assumption of inappropriate roles. As mentioned, they also value their lifestyle outside of work, be it family, sports, specific hobbies, or the arts. Like their Strategist cohorts, Tactician entrepreneurs may be workaholics, but unlike the Strategists, Tacticians focus on the more enjoyable aspects of life—while the Strategist entrepreneurs may still be burning the midnight oil.

Tacticians derive a special kind of enjoyment from anything beautiful expressed in form, color, and sound. They are sensitive to artistic nuances, and they like to do things gracefully. Not surprisingly, therefore, Tactical entrepreneurs tend to value their personal appearance with a fashionable, personalized, and color-coordinated style.

Tacticians are gutsy; they demonstrate confidence when others are floundering. They personify their own values and goals. In fact, they enjoy being the bon vivant, both at work and at play. They are likely to stay up late, burn the candle at both ends, and get things done their way.

Expectations

Typical Tactician entrepreneurs march to the beat of a different drummer. What Tacticians expect and set out to achieve is driven neither by experimental concepts nor time-tested organizational parameters and boundaries, for Tacticians are unencumbered by the trivia of the organization and the unrealistic dreamers on space patrol. Rather, the expectations of Tactician entrepreneurs are driven by value created for the all-important client/customer. Introverted Tacticians, especially, tend to be perfectionists to the point of masochism, practically living and breathing for the recognition clients and customers give them for being able to consistently deliver superior performance. Extraverted Tacticians, on the other hand, while always putting on their best face and charming their clients, may delegate more than they should; as a result, they may not always deliver the very best product. But introverted Tactician entrepreneurs are personally involved out of habit in ensuring that quality is delivered.

Tacticians expect their people to be highly responsive not only to the customers but also to one another. As a successful market-driven Tactical leader said, "If we treat each other as well as we do our valued customers, those who buy our services will always consider us superior to the competition." The element of time is important for Tactician entrepreneurs. Ideally, they want to accomplish everything yesterday. They have neither tolerance nor patience with second best or mediocrity, unless they view their operation as making a fast buck and then vanishing.

One of the charming traits of these entrepreneurs is their sense of egalitarianism. They tend to freely cross over hierarchical boundaries; they go directly to the source whether it be within or outside of their organization, and they expect their people to have a similar attitude. Nothing is impossible, and no one will prevent them from achieving what they want. Naturally, Tacticians expect everyone to hone their skills and constantly refine their capabilities so as to serve the clients and customers with increased precision and capability.

Lifestyle

The everyday lifestyle of Tacticians in many ways can be compared with hunters: They are constantly searching for opportunities to outshine everyone. Hence there is no such thing as an "everyday lifestyle" for Tacticians; rather their style is one of immediately responding to changes in the environment and taking advantage of circumstances before others even notice. One of the Tacticians we worked with over a long period defied all the established rules of the automotive industry by representing noncompeting manufacturers and securing seven different competitive dealerships in the same town. Being a masterful negotiator and never taking no for an answer, he negotiated his way into the hearts of manufacturers of American, Japanese, Korean, and German automobiles.

The everyday lifestyle is more like a journey for Tacticians than for any of the other entrepreneurs. They cannot and will not find themselves in a stabilized position where business is conducted as a matter of routine. It is useful to know that Tactician entrepreneurs thrive on chaos, as there are times when they may create a little discord here and there to keep themselves entertained. We also know they derive a certain amount of satisfaction in rebelling against or deviating from established norms.

Tacticians seem to have an unlimited capacity for enjoying festive occasions. Indeed, they are the great celebrators of life; they enjoy dressing up and being in the midst of activities. Do not be surprised to find that Tacticians are creative artists, enjoying life as entrepreneurs, masters of ceremonies, and centers of attention.

Two of the most fascinating Tactician entrepreneurs with whom I have been privileged to work with were Beverly Trupp and David Tieger.

▼ Beverly Trupp, CEO of Color Design Art, Inc.

In her mid-thirties, Beverly Trupp left behind her childhood dream job as a schoolteacher to work day and night building what is now known as Color Design Art, Inc., perhaps the most successful interior decorating firm for the leading developers in the United States. Her success is a living example of the American way of life. She developed her company while she was living in a modest apartment and teaching school, and ended up in a spectacular office in Pacific Palisades, where Sunset Boulevard meets the Pacific Ocean.

It is important to understand that background determines expectations. Beverly's early years went from sweet to sour. Until age six, she was encouraged to live life for all it was worth, loving it as provided by her parents. She recalls, "I remember the parties, going to the bowling alleys with my dad and singing 'You Are My Sunshine.' There was a real sense of specialness during those six years." Then there was a divorce. "I became an adult overnight. I was a caretaker of both my mother and my little sister from the time I was eight years old." Her mother had rejected her husband, and now Beverly became fearful that she, too, would be asked to leave.

In those early years, she learned to be responsible and worked toward her own independence. "I had this dream to be a teacher, so I played school; I practiced; I was a leader; and I was the baseball captain." Eventually, she graduated magna cum laude from the University of Southern California and was recognized for her unusual gifts in working with children.

Long before she reached her teens, Beverly had become an independent person, relying upon herself and her own judgments because her initial and traditional support systems had been ripped away. Any time it was suggested that there was something she could not accomplish, Beverly rose to the challenge and exceeded expectations. At sixteen, she told a girlfriend, "Sure, I know how to drive your car." With Beverly behind the steering wheel, they came to a turn, and not knowing how to use the steering wheel, she crashed! Even so, Beverly's response to a challenge remains, "Sure, I can do it, " and it was with this attitude that she entered the business world.

In 1970, a real estate developer happened to visit her apartment and was so impressed by the interior decoration that he asked Beverly if she could decorate twelve new model homes under construction. Her answer: "Sure, I can do it." She did it successfully, and from that point on, Beverly rose to become one of the most sought-after decorators in the business.

Bear in mind that she is a Tactician who learned early in life that she could not trust people and therefore had to differentiate herself and create her own values. "Everything my family did, I did the opposite. My mother smoked. I never did. My mother drank too much. I didn't have a drink until I was twenty-five. There was no religion in my home. When I was six years old, I took myself to Sunday school. I had something in me that was going to be separate and valuable, and I knew I did not have to do what everybody else does. I knew I would make up my own life. There was this other thing in me that said, Whatever you do, you have to be the best. That is a drive in you which can really wear you out."

She went on to explain that because of her dedication and work ethic, she knew going in that she would have to retire in her mid-fifties in order to retain her sanity—which she did. It goes without saying that Beverly was initially a workaholic, but more than that, she also had a clear sense of destiny. People have always played a large role in her life. "I have felt for the people working for me. They had to understand where we were going. I knew they needed a leader who would guide them in the right direction so they would be relieved of the opportunity to be in charge of their own fate. I had vision, I had goals, and I always spoke the truth. I never closed my door, ever, and I was always there for everyone. I didn't keep files because I always knew where to go for information."

As a Tactician entrepreneur, Beverly had no use for titles, and when she brought people into the firm they became members of a family. Her philosophy was clear and to the point: "People would use titles for power instead of building relationships and be given a false sense of authority. You earn respect and you earn it from your people. If people don't respect you, you have a problem, and a title can't remedy that."

Frequently, Beverly was accused of being a benevolent dictator. She didn't mind because, as she explained, "If the firm was going to go anywhere and create exceptional value, everybody would need to march to the same music." Yet she was humble: "I know I'm not holier than thou." She needed to set the highest standard she could for performance; she had no need for planning the longer growth cycles of the firm. The success of her firm can be attributed solely to its ability to create aesthetic value. Hence the nature of the business was such that it needed to be impulse driven, for no two assignments would ever be alike. In defiance of the strategic planning gurus, Beverly said, "It was really easy for us not to look at how to grow the company. Our challenge was to separate ourselves from our competitors and create more value than anyone, allowing us to charge more because we had a depth in our work that no one else could offer. Even today, four years after my departure, the firm is virtually without competition."

Beverly adheres to what she calls "the highest possible moral ethic." "I never looked behind me," she said. "I never had to worry about what I said to someone, because they all knew that eventually the business would be in their hands. They all knew that one day I would leave." Clearly, Beverly was at her best in building up the firm and then departing when she no longer could enjoy her personal, albeit somewhat undisciplined, touch with people.

Beverly's style is still that of a teacher. She prides herself on two things: attracting individuals who are likely to be highly successful and providing learning experiences for her employees so that over time they can do a better job than she did. Two examples: Several years ago, she hired a young girl to cook lunches for the staff so that no time would be wasted going to restaurants. The young lady did her job well and became a member of the family. Early on, she became interested in the design work done by some of the top-flight people in the firm, and they in turn were impressed by her questions and suggestions. In order to help her become upwardly mobile, Beverly decided to promote her to receptionist, where she failed miserably. Beverly's reaction to the declining performance of her new receptionist was not to let her go as other CEOs might have done but to cycle her into other work in the firm. Today she is one of the top designers at Color Design Art.

Next to her home in Malibu, Beverly had a guest house. She decided to hire a young couple, newly emigrated from Poland, to take care of her property, with the husband also working as a chauffeur. But it turned out the wife couldn't cook and the husband was "a flying maniac," according to Beverly. Being concerned with people, she felt so miserable about her bad decision that she transferred her driver to the warehouse. Over a short period, Beverly found out that her suicidal driver was extremely talented in creating children's bedrooms and other artistic projects. Today he is very sucessful as a CPA. Beverly said, "Only because you pay attention to people and allow them to express themselves, you say 'Wow, this person can do this and that person can do that.' So at Color Design Art, no one remains stuck in one spot. People move around as much as they want. If you want to grow, I will do whatever I can to support you. My role is to raise people up to new heights all the time."

True to form, Beverly is a hands-on person. She wants people to work harmoniously together, and she abhors conflict. Yet when people begin to sabotage one another, she brings them into the conference room and stays there until a solution is agreed upon. Even though such exercises clearly are necessary, they take up a huge amount of Beverly's energy.

Early in her career, she developed a deep respect for people. "We have learned to establish relationships in our company where diversity becomes our strength." Beverly once worked with someone who was so structured that she could never respond to anything spontaneously. "I think I probably was abusive to her. I was constantly demanding for her to do things that were totally against her nature, and for years I could not understand why she couldn't do it my way. The good news is that she didn't quit. I learned to respect her style and stopped asking her to be like me. Her niche became marketing, our clients love her, and she loves to be on the firing line all by herself."

In reflecting on how she got the company off the ground, Beverly explained that she worked seven days a week, "from morning till sleep," fifteen hours per day with no time off during the first seven years. "I loved it, I was passionate about it. First, I had started a business I had never worked in, so I had no experience. The challenge consumed all of me, and everything fed on itself to the point of being very dynamic. Second, I went to great lengths to hire the right people and train them. And third, I realized I wasn't too smart, because I had to do everything myself. I would sign every check for years, and, to the extreme, I knew every minute detail of everything in the firm. Finally, I realized that I could not continue to do that and had to learn how to delegate. I was driven to learn just like when I was a teacher, and then I found that when I began to relax, I got bored."

With the aid of time, Beverly learned that she could not be all things to all people and that she needed to become, in her own words, "a smart servant," both to people within the organization and to clients and customers. "CDA went from no repeat to total repeat. We simply don't lose clients, because of our devotion and commitment to them and the service we provide."

It has been interesting to follow Beverly over these years. What is not atypical is a hands-on Tactical operator; Beverly could cope better with the organization when it was small, unpredictable, and challenged with delivering superior performance, often under adverse circumstances. With growth came the infiltration of organizational development; toward the end of her tenure with the firm, Beverly appeared to remove herself from the organization simply because its size and the increasing skill level of her key people, reduced her opportunities to be hands-on. In her own words, "The company needed new growth and new leadership because it had peaked. But you know, how many more times are you going to do that? Forget it. For me it was like, I've done that, been there, and have that T-shirt. It is time for me to move on into another life and allow the company to grow, too."

Her focus and emphasis from the time she was eight years old has been one of personal mastery; when she was at peak performance and did not know how to improve, the inevitable boredom set in. Had there been a better or higher awareness of her need for involvement in operations, it is quite conceivable that she would have stayed. However, her brother, Don, who had worked with her for years, is now president, twelve years her junior, and is managing the now well-established firm on a day-to-day basis.

Although Beverly is extraverted, she works quietly and comfortably alone or with a few select and trusted people. She has a relentless desire for quality, and when people do not meet her expectations, she can be difficult to get along with.

A sensing person in two dimensions, Beverly nevertheless has intuitive capabilities. She has an unusual capacity to work with theories, concepts, and ideas and tends to believe that nothing is good enough; everything must constantly be improved. Although more concrete than abstract, her great strength is to take concepts and move them toward reality, using her street smarts. She is also a realist as a result of her life's experiences; she therefore assumes that people need to be both abstract and concrete, unusual traits for a Tactician.

Although she is values driven, Beverly is a Feeler and therefore a high-touch, caring individual who cannot function well when people are in conflict. These values, however, are augmented by the fact that she is a reasonable person who expects people to accommodate and support one another.

Beverly is only slightly more perceiving than she is structured; therefore, she cannot concentrate on too many projects at once; she needs to finish one project at a time. Somewhere in her life, she has learned to trust schedules and methodologies. There is a certain theme in her work, and variations on that theme come naturally to her.

A born optimist, Beverly can endure a great deal of ambiguity and frustration without losing her sense of balance. The fact that she is a reasonably carefree person has stood her in good stead throughout her adult life.

Unlike many of her contemporaries, Beverly is extremely decisive; people know where they stand with her, and she does not procrastinate. She readily admits that in her younger days the sheer velocity of her decisions at times was accomplished at the cost of not collecting sufficient data.

Beverly tends to lead by setting examples of kindness and understanding. You will not find her charging up a hill with a flag, expecting the troops to follow. Rather, she takes a personal interest in each member of her "family" and their professional development, and naturally expects everyone to maximize their own personal growth potential.

Beverly's values are directed toward giving people a real sense of fulfillment and pleasure in their work. Throughout the interview, her dislike for organizational structure shone through. One of her staff said, "Anytime you ask Beverly for a decision, she'd much rather give you information." She does not believe in asserting her will on other people. Her bias is for action, not philosophy.

As the company grew, Beverly grew disappointed because she could no longer be all things to all people; there simply wasn't enough of her to go around. She explained, "As the company exceeded fifty employees, I felt more and more useless because I don't like structure. I don't like all the layers. As long as I was creating and doing things, life was good. When you have to fit yourself into a system, I'm not good at that. I need to be able to create working relationships unencumbered from forced routine. I was not in touch with all the people as much, and where my strength lies is to know every person and to know exactly what they need to do that day and to encourage them and to say, 'Wow, that's a great idea. Go do it.'

The schoolteacher in me says I can handle up to thirty-five people, but the minute you cross over to fifty it is too many layers and I'm just a poor leader. I felt like a fish out of water. I was definitely not being productive and at my best. I had people doing things, I had managers and all that, but I just sort of disappeared. I lost my personal touch."

When Beverly was no longer able to grow the people who were growing the business, and she had lost her capacity to influence people positively, her work life ceased to be fun. Moreover, with systems and routine replacing the thrill of risktaking, her sense of enjoyment vanished. Realizing that she had come to the end of her working journey, she gracefully exited her business to spend time in nature and being active in her church.

▼   David Tieger, CEO of Gemini Consulting

David is a tactician entrepreneur with a strong bent toward strategic alertness. After acquiring the firm in 1973, David ressurected the consulting firm United Research. Years later, United Research acquired the Mac Group and the joint entity became known as Gemini Consulting. The business grew from annual revenues of $600,000 in 1973 to $540 million in 1994 making it, under David's leadership, the fastest growing major consulting firm in the world.

A business giant in his own lifetime, David was born in New Jersey to German and Austrian parents. His father owned and operated one of the most renowned restaurants in the state at that time, frequented by people from all walks of life. David's father, an intellectual at heart, could not afford to be educated at an institute of higher learning during his formative years, yet his passion for university teaching stayed with him all his life and was transferred to his sin long before David received his formal education. David explains, "By the time I was three years old, I knew I would attend Cornell University."

Clearly out of the ordinary, David's parents placed exceptionally high demands on him, causing David, in turn, to regard himself as a free and independent performer. Said David, "My father used life and the restaurant as a university—customers included leaders in business, government, and the famous artists and prize fighters of the time."

One such frequent visitor to the restaurant was Bill Bristol, the CEO of Bristol-Myers, and David explains, "My father wanted me to be at ease with anyone. He was fascinated by Mr. Bristol, and he told me to go over and say hello to him. When I objected, he said, 'David, Mr. Bristol is a gentleman; if you miss the opportunity to introduce yourself to him, there will be a piece missing from your education.' I walked over to Mr. Bristol, who rose from his chair to greet me. From him I learned that whenever anyone approached me, I would rise and remain standing until they would either sit down with me or leave. That way other people would always feel that our meeting was important to me."

Not surprisingly, David's strong lifelong work ethic was developed and shaped at a young age. "By the time I was fifteen years old, it was nothing to work twenty-four hours straight into the night and then continue working the next day. While I was reared to value being the best I possibly could be—through truth, discretion, honor, and duty—I was also reared to work hard."

It came naturally to David to have a high regard for the human dignity of people at every level of society, or as he expressed it, "I learned to honor human values and to shun arrogance." There were two beds in his room; "I would wake up and sleeping next to me might be a homeless person, a prize fighter, an artist, or a businessman invited to stay by my father. My father taught me to love the common man and to realize that small people in any organization can make a huge difference in the success or failure of any enterprise."

The foregone conclusion in everything and anything David undertook was "to deliver." Whatever commitments he made, the outcome had to meet the highest possible standards. In school, the only grade acceptable to his parents, and thus to David, was an "A". "I was expected to perform constantly. At the age of two, it was expected that I use the appropriate knife and fork and never leave the table without saying 'Thank you.' By the age of five, I was expected to name, as best I could, one headline from that day's *New York Times*, "OpEd" page. On reflection, I am not sure I ever was a kid—at least not in the traditional sense."

David is an unusually gifted person. In large part, his success can be attributed to his sense of omnipresence. He is a performer with the flair and creativity of an artist. He enjoys a heightened sense of vision, taste, touch, smell, and hearing. When he works with people, he listens for what they intend to communicate beyond what is actually said. He observes everything happening around him. He picks up on even the slightest cue, and nothing seems to escape his attention. His need for structure is minimal. He responds with ease and in a split-second; by instinct he will know what to do. When the sky is falling in, he never loses his composure. The unexpected is a way of life for David. "I have learned to take nothing for granted. I am astutely aware of the fact that, when people plan, the gods laugh!"

The significance of aesthetics is reflected in whatever David touches, be it at the intellectual, audio, or visual level. The Gemini offices in Morristown, New Jersey, are a case in point. The office environment in so uniquely designed that, frequently, Gemini was selected over major competitors such as McKinsey, the Boston consulting group, Arthur Anderson, and others, for large complex consulting projects. The message David communicated was one of superior capabilities in terms of people, their work environment, and their ability to deliver—to the point of exceeding expectations.

Given his strategic alertness, David is both a highly sensitive and self-critical individual. In his many years as a CEO, one of his great attributes has been that of positively and constructively affecting people in his firm and, through them, adding human, operational, and economic value to client organizations that few, if any, competitor could match.

David's personal work style is chameleon-like in that he is flexible in his approach to meeting objectives: He is omnipresent, connecting with people "everywhere and at once," yet always alert and keenly aware of his priorities. He trusts his impulses and, in short-cycle situations, that is when there is a need for fast action, David is second to none. He has an unusual capacity to quickly comprehend unmet client needs along with understanding the direction required to resolve highly complex problems. It should come as no surprise, therefore, that David was born a great negotiator.

When he acquired United Research in 1973, he borrowed $500,000 to "get the show on the road." During the first year, thirteen of the original team of fifteen consultants did not meet the new standards and were asked to resign. David quickly realized that three years prior to his acquisition of the firm a number of the most talented consultants had resigned voluntarily. He contacted them all and promptly rehired seven of the most successful individuals. These consultants became the cornerstone of the newly formed entity. David went to great lengths to create and articulate a vision, along with a career path, for each of the key people. From the moment they were engaged, they were committed to bringing United Research, and thereafter Gemini, into a leading position in the industry. In less than twenty years, David and his team increased annual sales revenue by more than 9,000 percent. "I felt I had a clear vision of what the future could be," David explained. "Rather than being an 'also ran' in the tradition-bound disciplines of strategy systems, technology-focus, and human resources, United Research became the first and leading consultancy to understand the interrelationship of all of these disciplines in creating wealth for client organizations. The learning and implementation of these strategies was under constant scrutiny and improvement. However, the fundamental concept of creating wealth for clients never changed."

In keeping with the values instilled in him during his formative years, David knew never to settle for anything but the best. In the early 1990's Gemini was widely recognized as having masterfully exploited the most relevant niche in the industry and, as such, having earned a leadership position. In reflecting on how it all came together, David explained, "When we started, no one was paying attention to us, and we loved being in that position. We would say, 'Let's keep our competitors' awareness of what we are doing low until we get large enough to go toe-to-toe with the most powerful competitors—and then win!' During that twenty year period, we became the fastest growing consulting firm in the world. We expanded at a compound growth rate of 35 percent per year. First we were among the top 100 of all consulting firms in the world, then among the top 40 and, by 1994, we were among the top 10 and receiving more competitive attention than we wanted!" Until his retirement in 1995, Gemini continued to be a stellar performer.

David's approach to life is an extension of his persona, strong value orientation, and personal commitment in everything he undertakes. He is obsessed with being sovereign and delivering uncompromising quality in everything he does. According to David, "Each day you fight to be the best you can possibly be and, when you go to sleep at night, you think you have moved forward. Then you wake up the next morning to find yourself pushed back to square one by the forces of mediocrity. The pursuit of excellence is a daily battle." When he acquired United Research, the firm was out of cash and lacked steady sources of income. It was at that time that he negotiated their first contract with a triple A–rated utility company without compromising the quality of work he wanted his firm to deliver. Other, more established, consulting firms had made multiple attempts to secure the assignment from the utility company to no avail. With his team, David designed a solution both bolder and superior to any presented by the competition. His proposal was favorably received, but he was asked to provide a very significant discount on what would be a much needed and very prestigious assignment for his firm. Throughout the difficult negotiations, David stuck to his principle of "one price, one quality" and explained that if the price were to be reduced, then the scope of the consulting work would also have to be pared down, and that the results would not be of the magnitude the client needed. The CEO of the utility company responded: "Your competition is banging at my door to work for free just for the prestige and exposure of working with us, and you want to get paid—even for the initial study!" David stood his ground, not knowing whether his new firm would be able to survive without this assignment. He knew that a compromise on his part could not provide the quality needed to deliver the best possible solution. On Christmas morning, David's telephone rang; the CEO of the utility company called, and announced, "Merry Christmas, David. You got the job at your price."

David cannot be a passive observer. He thrives on translating ill-defined abstractions into concrete action. His contribution to the consulting industry will inevitably succeed him. As David explained, "Whenever the leading consulting firms in our industry began to imitate what we did, we decided that it was time to move on and to redefine the rules of the game one more time—this was at the heart of my initiating Gemini." And he concluded, "Perhaps my greatest strength is to turn dreams into reality and to create wealth for client companies."

CHAPTER FIVE

THE STRATEGIST

Holding onto advantages
may cause opportunities
to get lost.
—Olaf Isachsen

It is likely that the majority of entrepreneurs in the world are Strategists, for they have nowhere else to go with their many ideas for new and promising ventures. Strategists distinguish themselves by living both their personal and professional lives in the belief that what conceptually can be created can at some point be implemented—which may or may not be the case. However, there are times when they lose the patience to bring their dreams to fruition. What fascinates them is the idea and the challenge to create something new. Do not be surprised, therefore, if the Strategist entrepreneur has an insatiable need for accomplishment. Moreover, it is useful to realize that for these entrepreneurs, accomplishments are primarily "head trips." Once they understand how to achieve whatever they are setting out to do, they lose interest in the daily routine and execution of ideas. Strategists prefer to be conceptualists, not relegating themselves to the minutiae of routine and "business as usual."

They tend to be fiercely competitive, and their toughest competitors all too often turn out to be themselves. Strategist entrepreneurs are always searching for what "to be" and are not particularly interested in what "to do." Above all, they seek rational solutions; they have a compulsion to know why things are the way they are and happen the way they do.

It is interesting to know that Strategist entrepreneurs consider themselves to be quite accommodating, understanding, and empathetic, but at times those with whom they interact experience them as hard, cold, and calculating. Moreover, Strategists are not particularly well known for their patience, and they do not suffer fools gladly. One of the entrepreneurs we interviewed told us about his frequent prayer: "Lord give me patience, but do it now."

The word *imagineering* must have originated with a Strategist entrepreneur. He or she stays focused on the new ideas and concepts that spark their imagination, leaving items of less interest in an incomplete blur. They habitually are quite selective in what they choose to perceive, as they chiefly want to channel their energies in directions that first are fascinating and second, profitable. Unlike Administrator entrepreneurs, they are like butterflies: They like to "flutter by" many opportunities and challenges—often on a wing and a prayer and frequently with limited information. Expect especially the highly extraverted Strategist entrepreneurs to work from untested concepts and badly articulated hunches, not succeeding at the rate anticipated. Hence, not surprisingly, the amount of risk these entrepreneurs assume sometimes can get them into trouble and unanticipated losses.

The prosperity, creature comforts, and high standard of living enjoyed in our society can in no small way be attributed to thousands of Strategists and their willingness to take risks along with their ability to persevere even after short-term losses and interim failures. They are relentless, around-the-clock workaholics, driven to direct all available energy and imagination toward achievement. As one of our interviewees said, "I work at work and then I work at play as well." He admitted that he found it difficult to enjoy himself when involved in activities not related to work one way or another.

Strategists are fascinated by "back of the envelope" ideas, to the point of obsession. Hence, as no stone is too small to be unturned, no challenge is too minuscule to be explored and no opportunity too uninteresting to be considered. As might be expected, Strategists tend to be more polyactive than single-minded, typically taking on many endeavors simultaneously. Their need to forever search for something new is deeply embedded in their personality: After all, if there are no problems to be solved, what then is the purpose of a work life?

Do not be upset if a Strategist entrepreneur appears arrogant. Frequently they are unaware of their tendency to be aloof, off somewhere in their intellectual space; for they arrive at the future first, and understand concepts and ideas long before us mortals. Foresight for them is vital; theory captivates their imagination. Clearly, they are at their best when they are scheming, contemplating, and planning.

Typical Strategist entrepreneurs tend to excel at determining where to direct scarce resources. They enjoy formulating, more than implementing, strategies. The more complex their world, the more fulfilled they are. They are masterful in marshaling and directing resources toward the highest and best results. The price Strategists invariably have to pay for their orientation is that they tend to be lousy Tacticians; they are more gifted at designing an organization than working with its moment-by-moment aspects.

Extraverted Strategist entrepreneurs enjoy their capacity to delegate because it frees them from attention to details. There are times, however, when their propensity to delegate can boomerang and eventually cause declining performance. Introverted Strategist entrepreneurs, on the other hand, have to pay attention to details, at times micromanaging to such an extent that greater opportunities may be put on the sidelines. Moreover, it is not easy for introverted Strategist entrepreneurs to delegate because they believe no one can do the work better than they. Inherent in the successful pursuit of entrepreneurship is the need for ego gratification—and Strategists derive great satisfaction from demonstrating how brilliant they are from the action they initiate.

Role

Strategist entrepreneurs tend to view themselves as unusually gifted in taking charge. Their natural tendency is to assume leadership, particularly in unknown and high-risk situations where the safety net of day-to-day routine has not yet been installed. However, we lesser souls sometimes find it difficult to follow them into the unknown.

Strategist entrepreneurs are open to change. Indeed, they are the change masters, so they can easily be intellectual dilettantes and lose touch with day-to-day reality. Strategists are lifelong learners who quickly lose interest and search for new adventures when there is no more new learning to be done. Be alert: They tend to be autonomous; although modern-day business calls for team building, do not count on Strategists to join any crowd. They may play along with the team for the purpose of achieving interim goals and objectives and gaining better knowledge and adequacy, but they are not likely to enthusiastically join any team effort. They sometimes find it difficult to listen to others, especially about subjects in which they have no interest, and their attempts to appear polite, empathic, and understanding seem false.

The role of Strategist entrepreneurs in any working situation is to constantly be different and sometimes even contrary, for they know they add originality to a world dominated by conformity and stagnation.

Modus Operandi

The modus operandi of Strategist entrepreneurs is to preserve the freedom of increased options. They need freedom to intellectually soar, to view the world from conceptual perspectives, not from predetermined angles. From time to time, they may become fascinated with a particular aspect of a given situation and direct their entire attention there, failing to see the whole picture. It is difficult for Strategists to leave the domain of translating ideas and concepts into realities, of "figuring things out." They rely on more grounded, detail-oriented people for the day-to-day routine work. They may not particularly enjoy these colleagues, but experience has proven that the two of them working together understand and respect each other's unique strengths. Strategists are so absorbed in what they do that they risk living only for work. Family and friends frequently find themselves in a secondary position. Strategists cannot understand that others do not direct as much energy and effort into their work as they do. It is useful to recognize that Strategists are so demanding of themselves that they may extend the same expectations and pressure to others with quite different life agendas.

Values

Strategists place more value on analysis, exploration, and the intellect than do the other three entrepreneurial types. They view their world of thinking and turning insights into new opportunities as synonymous with progress and achievement. Moreover, they value objectivity and gaining knowledge so much that they are at a loss when others rely more on their emotions than on logic. Unlike other entrepreneurial types, Strategists enjoy problem solving and mental gymnastics as much as or more than merely achieving predetermined goals. For them, framing problematic situations into new and more productive concepts is extremely gratifying. People who do not understand their motivation and orientation may be upset by their flexibility. Certainly they do not work within a predictable, systematic routine.

Strategist entrepreneurs enjoy being able to influence people. They also usually enjoy being influenced by others. On the other hand, when they are on a roll, it may take some time for their momentum to wind down and for them to be open to new input.

These entrepreneurs value debate. They can discuss anything with anyone without taking themselves too seriously. To talk out of both sides of their mouth at the same time is, for them, natural, invigorating, and fun, especially for the extraverted types. Others may feel squelched by this behavior.

Strategists place a high value on will, for they feel they can will themselves into whatever they want. They enjoy a kind of intellectual elasticity and therefore can waltz in and out of situations, even without a partner.

Expectations

The expectations of Strategist entrepreneurs are straightforward: Do as I say and not necessarily as I do. They believe that they know what is best for everyone and that they can charm people into doing just about anything. In fact, they expect to be admired, loved, and worshipped by whomever they work with because their contribution is intellectually superior, unique, and more valuable than anyone else's. Over time, though, they are likely to realize that their charm has its limits.

Strategists expect people to work intelligently but not necessarily hard. That is not to say that they do not personally adhere to the Protestant work ethic. They know, however, that exceptional results are produced only by exceptional individuals, not by followers. Implicitly, Strategist entrepreneurs understand and appreciate Carl Jung's observation: "As any change must begin somewhere, it is the single individual who will experience it and carry it through."

Unlike Administrator entrepreneurs, Strategists don't necessarily believe that "everyone should do their *duty*," because the term duty implies the inability to intellectualize and, worse yet, the tendency to accept the status quo. Indeed, they abhor the herd instinct. More like hunters than gatherers, Strategists enjoy the journey, not necessarily the destination. As the French writer Marcel Proust said, "The real voyage of discovery consists not in seeking new landscapes but in having new eyes."

Strategists, then, are unencumbered thinkers who challenge established processes for the purpose of creating more, better, faster, and less costly value for their clients and customers. (An example of that kind of achievement is evidenced in the increased capacity and decreased cost of computers.) Indeed, Strategist entrepreneurs expect to be respected for their unique capacity to be trailblazers and to set the trend for the future, for they hope to make a difference of lasting value both for themselves and a larger constituency.

Lifestyle

The everyday lifestyle of Strategist entrepreneurs is first and foremost affected by their belief that there are never enough hours in the day to do everything they want to do. Highly energetic, it is not unusual for Strategist entrepreneurs to rise before dawn and return home very late. They never cease to explore, study, read, and stay informed on whatever is important to them. Do not expect to find them on the baseball diamond, in the gym, or at public events. They prefer to be at work with an occasional passing thought for an outside event than to be at the event itself, thinking about work.

There may be times when Strategists venture out to do something that is good for their health and well-being. These tend to be highly individualized activities; Strategists enjoy competing against themselves more than against others, believing that "Anything I can do, I can do better." Hence, competitive sports typically involve non-team-oriented activities such as golf, skiing, and tennis.

On an everyday basis, then, the Strategist entrepreneur intellectually traverses endless new terrain, returning enriched in experience, knowledge, and new perspectives.

▼ John Dean, CEO of Silicon Valley Bank

Fewer people come into this world as a leader, but John Dean, a banker and a Strategic entrepreneur, did. As far back as John can remember, he always wanted to take the lead. He has an insatiable need to climb mountains, but as soon as he is on a peak, he has no capacity to enjoy the view and his achievement. Rather, he slides into the nearest valley as fast as he can and gears up for his next climb. "Damn the torpedoes and full speed ahead" is John's motto. For him, the past is uninteresting and irrelevant. Though he may be viewed more as an intrapreneur (one who brings about change within in an organization) than an entrepreneur, John is certainly entrepreneurial and has reached financial independence.

At a very young age, John developed tremendous self-confidence. Whatever happened, he always needed to understand the meaning of events. His energy level has always been high. He is up and out of the house by six every morning, and he accomplishes more in one day than normal individuals accomplish in one week.

Whatever John takes on becomes his crusade, and he gains the greatest satisfaction from solving problems where others have failed. He is a natural and independent leader who works exceedingly well with people but leans on them in order to effect the best possible outcome. He explained in one of our interviews, "I always need to chart my own course."

Fiercely independent, John nevertheless listens to people and appreciates their contributions. In the final analysis, though, he needs and wants to jump that last, crucial hurdle, make the critical decisions, and take full responsibility, whatever the outcome.

John was probably independent by the age of ten. His caring parents knew what they wanted for him, but he was determined to find his own way. So instead of getting an MBA, he joined the Peace Corps and gained experience of a different kind. Unlike the Administrator type, John strove to blaze his own trail independent of the past. As he moved toward the future, the horizon kept on shifting farther and farther away.

The word setback is not in John's vocabulary. There may be interferences in his quest for success, but he will never take no for an answer. He tends to pressure others relentlessly, which often causes them to shift position. Although he may be viewed as a loner in his thinking process, his work life has taught him that spectacular results are achieved by team efforts. When he took on the responsibility as CEO for Silicon Valley Bank, it was eminently clear to him that he would need a group of people who would honor their differences and make a uniform commitment to lift the organization by its bootstraps. No team is perfect, but John and his group increased bank stock from $8 to $24 within three years. Although these results are significant, John is strategizing for even higher achievements.

Comfortable working with people on a one-on-one as well as on a group basis, his self-imposed task is always to challenge the status quo. One of his top executives told me, "Anytime I have a conversation with John, two things happen: I walk out more challenged, and I know I'm damn good."

Anything routine deprives John of the best use of his time as the consummate problem solver, marshaling all the available resources to storm ahead. Moreover, he is the type of CEO who can accomplish many tasks simultaneously. Unlike the Administrator entrepreneur, he is unorthodox and pays little attention to formalized organizational hierarchies. Although clearly aware of being the ultimate decision maker, John can be found anywhere at any time in the bank interacting with people. As he said, "I don't care what level a person is at. He or she has something important to contribute. I'm fortunate in that I do have a genuine curiosity about other people."

John prefers a summary of ten issues to a multitude of details about one issue. Once he takes charge, he quickly delegates tasks and responsibilities to others. Although he empowers others, he has said, "You cannot empower before you have competence."

John perceives only moving targets. Anytime a member of his team achieves a goal, John creates a new goal, for he believes that capacity to perform is directly correlated to available challenges. Although he lives in the future, John knows that the daily work must be done. He knows how to comfortably involve himself with everyday issues: "I'm not their boss. Mine is more of a cheerleader role, because I'm their partner. Yet I consider myself a leader and I'm very results driven." When what needs to be done is clear, however, don't expect John to hang around, as his major contribution as a Strategic entrepreneurial CEO is always "what to be," not "what to do."

As a driven, objective leader, John nevertheless seeks to be sensitive and understanding. One imagines that John views himself as both a tough taskmaster and an encouraging coach, for he does not lead by command. With an exceptional capability for understanding the proper timing for any action, he will look people straight in the eye with both good and bad news. And he knows how to confront dysfunctional behavior while maintaining his respect for the person's integrity. "I set the example, and I need to be the highest standard of everything that exists in the bank," he said. He can express displeasure and anger, yet people still enjoy themselves in his presence.

High on John's agenda are integrity, fairness, and accountability. His integrity is driven by more than ethics alone. He believes that cutting corners and deriving personal benefits from one's position within an organization eventually tears the delicate fabric of trust, which is indispensable for the ultimate success of all involved. "I don't like people who are dishonest or deceiving," he said, "because then I don't know how to manage them."

Closely related to John's sense of integrity and honesty is his need for people to be accountable to themselves for whatever action they take. He considers being called upon to intervene extremely counterproductive: "If I'm hands-on with what you're doing, you're at risk because I haven't got time to do your job."

Flexibility and adaptation are ongoing themes in John's life, particularly when applied to his mental agility. At the age of nineteen, he found himself in France: "I marched with the crowd for de Gaulle and I marched with the crowd against de Gaulle. It was great." Whatever John sets his mind to do, he does with zest and passion. In his risktaking, he always exercises the full strength of his mind.

John is always willing to provide resources on any issue. "If you've got a problem, I'll listen and work with you. But if you are not willing to bring this issue to a resolution, then I am not willing to continue to assist you." He values expertise, and what precedes expertise is autonomy, an inquisitive nature, the ability to grasp concepts with ease, and an appreciation for intelligence and its appropriate use. He has always strived for excellence and he believes you never stop getting better and better. As the third child of seven and the oldest boy, he felt pressure to excel. "There was certainly a feeling on my part that no matter how well you did, you could have done better." John wondered if this is the reason that many of his siblings are over-achievers.

Without a doubt, John is strong and operates on many fronts simultaneously. But can he identify with the rest of us? Absolutely. John embraces the dignity of all individuals.

"I always think the odds are much in my favor," John said. That is, he mentally sets the stage for the best possible outcome. His expectations are very high and they continue to be high. It is important to note that John doesn't relax once he has reached a certain comfort zone. "I've come to the conclusion that I have to climb mountains and I'll never stop." He is continually searching for ways to improve his skills, seeking expertise in whatever he undertakes.

John assumes appropriate levels of risk and expects those with whom he works closely to do the same. "I love the fact that I have the ability to change things. I want to make sure that I'm adding value to this journey I'm on, without taking undue risks." John intuitively understands a quote from Santhanam C. Shekar: "By the time the rules of the game are clear, the window of opportunity will have closed."

Failure is not an option for John. If for any reason there is a backlash or unpleasant surprise, he confronts the situation and finds ways to change what does not work. He is a strong believer in changing circumstances, not people. For him, people are what they are. Moreover, he is aware of the power in leveraging his energies. Hence, he is willing to delegate and give people responsibilities, sometimes beyond their immediate capacity, allowing for both personal and professional growth.

Having learned to trust his gut instinct, John expects to make initial, hard decisions unflinchingly, even if he has to operate with insufficient data. He places a greater premium on intelligence than on demonstrated ability to perform within traditional parameters and creates an environment where differences among people are honored and the tough questions are asked without fear of reprisals. He also gives people full credit for their unique and often valuable contributions, encouraging and expecting them to celebrate early wins as long as they don't become enraptured by the view from the top of the mountain. His expectation that everyone on his team will strive to add exceptional value ultimately allows the bank to be the only financial institution capable of delivering a unique set of financial products and services to the high-tech industry and to some of the most sophisticated clients in the country.

However, John places the highest demands on himself. "Even today people expect a lot of me and I kind of like being in that position." His range of interests goes beyond family and business. "This is a great job for me, but what value am I contributing to humanity?" he said, demonstrating his willingness to ask tough, provocative questions. In fact, his work history provides evidence that he will never tolerate complacency and stagnation, that he will continue to grow, to give, and to get the most out of life. "I couldn't tell you at a young age that I wanted to be a bank CEO, because even today I tell people that I'm not sure that I know what I want to be. I just know that I very much enjoy what I'm doing right now and I always need to be challenged."

At work, he is like quicksilver, at times attempting to attend two meetings simultaneously. His mind is quick, and his ability to pick up the essentials without the irrelevant is so highly developed that he doesn't miss much.

A full-time lover and connoisseur of life, John's interests range from being with entrepreneurs and venture capitalists, to helping his daughter clean up her horse's stable, to attending the theatre as well as other performing events. He has a great capacity to network, especially with individuals important to the bank. For him, work never really ends, for he does not distinguish between work and private time. However, there are times when he totally tunes out to garden and/or be with his family. Although on the surface it may appear that he is a workaholic, he does not experience serious stress. Somehow, an internal signal tells him that the time has come to redirect his energy to his family, friends, and private pursuits. In the final analysis, family comes first: During a retreat with his key people, John had to take care of a family situation and explained that he would return to the session two hours later.

Although John takes his work and responsibility very seriously, he is nevertheless quite comfortable poking fun at himself. Also, he will go out of his way to demonstrate that he is prepared to devote time and energy to assist people when they need help. Clearly, he is both willing and able to subordinate his own agenda for the benefit of those for whom he is ultimately responsible.

John has created around him an aura of energy, mutual respect, involvement, commitment, and humor. As one of his team members said, "His passion for people is legendary. He is revered to a fault and creates an atmosphere that promotes respect by honoring our differences more than our similarities."

▼   Tony Spare, CEO of Spare, Kaplan, Bischel & Associates

In the sense that Tony Spare, an investor and a Strategist, was born an entrepreneur, it is not accidental that he is the CEO of a highly successful investment firm. In a period of two years, he and his partners grew the firm from investing $350 million to $2 billion for major corporations throughout the United States. Prior to his career as an entrepreneur, Tony was an impossible-to-manage chief investment officer for a major California bank.

As a Strategist entrepreneur, Tony's need for knowledge, as you would expect, is insatiable. He always focuses on what will be; he is a futurist. With a rich inner life, he spends more time thinking than talking to others. He describes himself as a person who knows the exact moment for appropriate action.

Tony's desk is a mess, and he judges time by his inner clock and his priorities, which remain somewhere between a mystery and an impulse driven by the circumstances of the moment. His awareness of and quest for understanding cutting-edge technology and what lies beyond that make him a natural leader. Above all, Tony values logic and the ability to reason, which empower him to have access to all significant information.

When he was a child, he and his father, an attorney, liked to have lengthy discussions—and just for the hell of it often took opposite points of view. These long discussions prepared Tony for the harsh realities of investing, and his independent spirit motivated him to become an entrepreneur. "It's an interest in not being part of the crowd, of thinking differently and being independent. For myself, there has never been a bell, a whistle, or a single event that has caused me to become an entrepreneur. There haven't been any of those life-changing 'seeing the light' moments. To the degree I am an entrepreneur, I have always been an entrepreneur."

Given his understanding of himself as an independent and intuitive thinker and because he is such a strong leader, Tony finds it best to manage himself. On par, his investment decisions generally outperform the competition. When the leadership team in the firm came to recognize and understand one another's styles and personality differences, conflicts disappeared, and Tony was granted even more authority and autonomy. He may not have a warm and fuzzy personality, but over the years he has proven to his co-workers his deep commitment to justice and fairness.

Fiercely independent, if deprived of tinkering with his lifelong investments, Tony will go elsewhere. Life without the opportunity to play a key role in the investment world is a life not worth living, for Tony knows that world extremely well and has no desire to live any other kind of life.

Tony can determine priorities and filter out what is unimportant. When he involves himself in an activity, it is with independence of mind, original thinking, and usually a contrarian perspective. In this way, he does his best work, remains in charge, and defends himself against time-wasting interference from others. He usually arrives at the future first, because today he can see in his mind how tomorrow's realities will evolve. He said, "It's not that everything is the same because it always changes. It's the ability to understand the important changes and separate the relevant from the irrelevant that counts, enabling me to move ahead. So the magic wand isn't to change anything; it is to continue the path as a kind of process and evolution that's already characterized."

As a Strategist, Tony's specific type is often referred to as the architect type; thus he may be identified as an architect of investment. He states, "Architects are funny beasts. To me, an architect is this balance between creativity and science engineering. It's doing the day-to-day as well as being able to view something of substance and permanence. If I can get that balance for the future and the creativity, and yet still make sure that the second floor is above the first floor and the roof fits and the girders fit, then I have a structure of substance—and that's what being an architect is."

Tony is an exceptionally tough entrepreneur, and as iron sharpens iron, he is forever honing his skills. Anyone in his organization not interested in and deeply committed to professional growth inevitably will fall by the wayside. Though they may not be fired, they will lose the opportunity to zoom into the future with Tony and the other high performers. A whiz with computers and a high-tech junkie, including satellite communication and wireless transfers, Tony keeps no calendar. Yet with amazing exactness, he knows where he will be just about every hour during the next thirty days. Perhaps he wants to retain his sense of privacy and only dole out information about his whereabouts to specific people on specific occasions.

During working hours, Tony is likely to be found in any office in quiet conversations with one or two of his trusted employees.

He is forever building new constellations and adding self-created new insights. His inner dialogue is rich and forever alert to change. He maintains what he considers to be a healthy skepticism of his own thoughts and ideas as well as those of others', yet he is always open to new ideas and new realities. He makes inferences and connections and draws conclusions faster than anyone in his firm. Although he listens to people, his attention span can quickly be reduced to half or less. If he listens to someone with nothing to say, Tony may be physically present but his mind is far away.

Because he dislikes fools, Tony may be viewed as arrogant and rude. But for him, simple issues are boring. His genius is having the ability to solve complex problems and to do so without introducing fickle human emotions. Yet he strives to be polite, considerate, and understanding, even though his facial expressions may indicate otherwise.

It is Tony's grasp of the future that accounts for his reputation, unbeatable track record, and great success. "Most of the time I try

not to live for today. I'm not trying to see the future. I really am trying to get out into the future and look backwards, which is different."
Hence he is more apt to leapfrog than pursue incremental planning,
being by nature a trailblazer. In order to collect his thoughts, Tony
maintains a second residence south of San Francisco where he can
often be found by himself surrounded by the latest information on
the economy, trends, and projected performance of selected companies.

Despite his capacity to juggle many thoughts and concepts, he has
a need to finish each project in a sequential order. Being highly perceptive, he values the quality of his work more than being on time.
Still, he performs superbly under pressure and if forced to make a
decision within a given time frame, he'll do it.

Being such a highly abstract person, Tony naturally likes to work
with possibilities. Although he can be quite decisive, there are times
he can drive more structured people crazy by perpetually coming up
with ideas from nowhere. Tony is unaware of the immediate world:
His car is full of newspaper clippings, journals, and electronic giz-
mos, and though from time-to-time he may clean it up, it is more as
a result of pressure from his family than his own need.

For Tony, "process" in a sense is "substance," as he is more interested in the circumstances creating substance than the substance
itself. His sense of timing combined with decisive action is perhaps
the key to his success. "I tend, as a manager, to keep as many balls in
the air as I can until it's time, and then I throw the ball as hard and
fast as I can. The timing has to be correct. I don't like decisions just
for the sake of making decisions." Therefore, the day-to-day mundane activities in his office warrant little if any of his attention.

In a moment of reflection, Tony told me that it is "too bad that I
can't do all of my ideas." He is exceptionally intuitive and always in
pursuit of intellectual, theoretical, and original ideas on just about
everything. A free spirit, he is energized by being casual and spontaneous, not systematic and scheduled.

Tony values conceptual clarity, and autonomy and independent
thinking are the *sine qua non* of conceptual clarity. Also valuing both
efficiency and effectiveness, he distances himself from incompetence.
Honesty, too, ranks high for Tony. Speaking of his employees, Tony
said, "The most important thing to me is honesty with themselves.

The whole purpose of going through any of the characterization tests is to better know yourself. I am a hardline rationalist. That's just what I am and how I operate. I'm an open book and I make myself known."

Tony not only values honesty, he also expects honesty in human interrelationships. "The most difficult people to deal with in any organizational setting, it seems to me, [are those] whose self-image is very different from the perceptions of others. Whether they intend to be dishonest with themselves or not isn't clear, but they are nonetheless never happy and satisfied because there's this constant conflict."

We know Tony has an excellent mind and is comfortable within his own mental domain. What does he think about his people skills? "I enjoy building the organization, being able to educate people, younger people attracting bright people to the organization who may or may not have much experience in investing per se but are inquisitive and thoughtful. When it comes to the other parts of the business, I like to attract people with a very consistent value system. We're honest and straightforward. We're not quick-buck artists. We're believers in serving clients . . . we all benefit from that financially. As an organization, there are really only two choices. You can either use clients or you can serve clients. Over time, service to the clients, doing something they need, something that's important to them, will benefit the entire organization. The organization will grow."

Tony expects people to know their strengths and their weaknesses. "What makes people successful is understanding their own strengths and being happy and focused on that." He added, "In putting an organization together, it's basically having different strengths [paired] with different weaknesses, but focus[ing] on the positive parts of the different strengths. Scalpels and broad axes are both cutting instruments, but you don't want to cut down trees with a scalpel and you don't want to have someone operate on you with a broad axe. They're both effective in their own ways and in their own uses."

Tony has learned to honor differences and ignore pressures of conformity. He is very much aware of the four basic human temperaments described in Chapter One, yet in his mind there is no excuse for people failing to use their gifts, for being unprepared and neglecting their homework, which, he believes, should not be done during working hours. Indeed, those who are looking to a long-term career with the company are expected to do their homework—at home.

Tony's firm is based on brain power. Hence, although Tony may be high-tech and high-brain, he is not a high-touch person. In other words, he will never be the world's greatest social director, but he will coach, help, and support people who want to be high performers in their respective field of expertise. His expectations are that the firm will be able to attract, develop, reward, and retain exceptional performers.

In Tony's domain, there is never enough information, hindsight, insight, or foresight to finish anything. He expects people to always be capable and flexible within the framework of insufficient information. Those who are frozen or opinionated are a constant irritant for him because of his high tolerance for uncertainty. He expects "the shape of things to come" to outpace "the way we were."

One trait that shines through is his unbending sense of justice, in which he places higher value on fairness and integrity than on the letter of the law. He has no intention of taking advantage of anyone, nor does he expect those with whom he works to ever derive personal benefit from any situation of the firm. In a business where the code of ethics is crucial for sustaining success, he will not accept any activity that could jeopardize the integrity and honor of the firm.

For Tony, "There's no single defining moment in anything. There's no compartmentalization of 'I have to go do this and that's a separate life from that.' It's all pieces of the same thing." This then is the key to Tony's consistent investment strategy and success. Indeed, he is a cool investor, beyond emotional disturbance, for he refuses to divide himself into a multitude of conflicting pieces. "What is stress to other people, to me is not stress. What is the work ethic to other people, I do not look at in those same terms. I once had somebody ask me how I deal with stress and my answer was, 'I *give* stress, I don't *deal* with stress.' That ends up meaning not that I intentionally inflict stress on other people, but if other people want to take it, fine."

A quiet, withdrawn person, Tony will be found neither with the "in-group" nor in the center of networking. He may seem shy, but he is not. He prefers to be with a few good friends, family, and his three partners. He enjoys working alone or meeting people on a one-to-one basis or in small groups. He is an early riser and connects with the world through CNBC every morning. Twelve-hour working days are his norm. He also disappears to his sanctuary south of San Francisco, where he continues to work alone, pondering issues and doing a lot of homework. He describes himself as not being very sociable and tending to "go off on my own with my wife Eleanor to do our own thing." All too often, people like Tony tend to be viewed as lacking in social skills, which is far from the truth. He also lacks interest in keeping up with current fashion. As a matter of fact, I cannot recall having worked with a more successful entrepreneur who unknowingly wore different colored socks! But Tony's limited need for sociability should not obscure the fact that he can be very sociable any time he chooses.

▼ Delores Kesler, Chair of Accustaff

Delores Kesler is perhaps one of the most unusual women of our times. Single-handedly, she conceived of establishing a temporary employment business that provides professional, not just clerical, help. Today she is chair of the fourth largest temporary employment firm in the United States, Accustaff.

Delores Kesler gained a great deal of self-confidence at an early age as a result of her father's natural inclination to be her mentor. He held a steady job with Southern Bell throughout his life, yet on the side he ventured into small entrepreneurial enterprises without much success. So when Delores was fourteen years old, she was exposed to her first entrepreneurial experience: "Dad was always running a little small business which never made any money. He had this need to be entrepreneurial, but I'm not so sure he put his heart into it. When I was fourteen years old, he bought a poultry farm and I got very involved in 4-H showing chickens and all that sort of thing. He really didn't have time to run the business, given his responsibilities at Southern Bell. So he turned the checkbook over to me and said we have $100 in the bank and $400 in bills. Even though I was very young, I didn't agree with the way my father ran the business, and with the checkbook in hand I was able to make the decisions which eventually made the business solvent. I'm very aware that I had the good fortune of having a father who placed a lot of faith in me. He died when I was only nineteen, but he had helped me to build enough self-esteem to know that whatever I really wanted to do I could accomplish. I remember when he took me fishing with his buddies. This experience provided a lot of exposure, and I became very comfortable around males. I didn't grow up [believing] that men do all the thinking and women do all the cooking."

By the time Delores was thirty-seven years old, she had enjoyed a mixed career working with everything from human resources to sales training and managing a small company for her aunt in providing specialists on a temporary basis to the medical business. "I always wanted to be in business for myself, but I neither had the training nor the education to venture out in a forceful fashion. I wanted to find something that would really interest me, and I was at an age where I either had to take a step into the unknown or continue being an employee. I knew I wasn't going to be very good in the typically female-owned businesses, such as running a flower shop, a dress shop, and a gift shop. I didn't know much about the temporary employment business, and yet I knew that what drives me is the pleasure of seeing something grow and develop, something that you feel you guided and you had the right process in place. I made a lot of mistakes, and yet I did a number of things innovatively and differently. I knew I needed some cash, and I ran into a bank president I'd gone to high school with and asked for a $50,000 loan. He said, 'I can't give you a loan, Delores. You have no security. You're going into an industry you don't know.' He told me his loan limit was $10,000 without security, and so I told him I would take it. A year later, I paid him back the $10,000, and he loaned me the $50,000 I needed to start the business."

Delores then spent a great deal of time thinking. She reviewed the competition carefully and came to the conclusion that all the temporary firms were basically in the staffing industry. Some of them tended to specialize in certain areas. She then developed a growth strategy where she entered into medical temporary employment, office staffing, technical staffing, computer analysts, engineers, financial planners, and CPAs. Within five years, Accustaff's revenue went from zero to $50 million. Being a highly rational person, Delores had neither an inclination nor a desire to rest on her laurels. At midlife, she decided to take a hard look at the performance of her firm in its competitive environment. "I needed something else to make my life more complicated. We were having fun making lots of money, but I kept asking myself, What do I really want to do? and I realized the only way to make an impact in the industry is to become a leader. It required that we would grow to well over $1 billion in annual revenue and operate in basically the entire United States. And so I said to myself, Well, it's impossible for me to go from $50 million to a billion without either going to the public or getting public funds. I eventually got together with three guys located in different parts of the United States in the same business as mine and put together an $80 million company. The largest player, Manpower, had enjoyed an annual compounded growth rate of 20 percent during the last fifteen years, allowing it to exceed $7 billion in annual revenue. Kelly Services was at $4 billion. When I looked at the competition, they were all generalists and served the lower ranks of the industry. Nobody was focusing on what we were, which was technical and specialty staffing. We ran the new operation until we got all the kinks out, put the infrastructure in place, got our economics in scale, downsized the other regional offices, made the headquarters here in Jacksonville, Florida; and I was the president and CEO. And we said, Now we are ready to go to the public market. Originally, we received $20 million, and we spent the money very well making acquisitions. We went back to the public market in September and raised over $100 million. And we were now at an annual revenue run rate of a little over $500 million. Practically overnight, we became a dominant player in the industry, and we have people knocking our doors down wanting a part of Accustaff."

Today, Accustaff is recognized as the leading temporary firm for providing highly competent personnel in technical and professional positions.

In reflecting on her unusual success, Delores commented, "The industry was asleep, and when I say 'we,' it was really I who kept saying, 'We need to do something to wake it up, and there needs to be competition for the five or six companies who have been asleep for a long time.' I reached out to other companies and merged with them.

By doing so, I discovered that there was a lack of leadership in the industry. Yet I could not be successful if I could not bring Accustaff up to a billion dollars of revenue in a year. So as we worked on the merger opportunities, I attracted leaders like myself and gave them enough opportunity to still have their entrepreneurial tendencies develop. Everyone told me I wasn't going to get the egos of the four guys satisfied, so I had to develop something that everyone had a stake in. The money was not the driver. My partners had to feel as if they could personally make a contribution and participate in the whole process."

Today Delores is not resting on her laurels: She will probably remain a workaholic for the rest of her life. It is through her efforts that she enjoys the fruit of her labor. She derives a great deal of satisfaction in sharing with would-be entrepreneurs. "It's hard to know what to do for an encore. I like most of all to be involved with things that have to do with entrepreneurs and maybe become some kind of a venture capitalist who could help other companies grow and develop as they are emerging. But also [I would enjoy] helping in some educational processes, because I had a tough time getting through school, and I really ended up with a company that did put me through school. That has been very important to me. So I want to give something back to some of the institutions [to overcome things] that I know were a hindrance, not only for me but for a lot of other people. They couldn't get the type of education they needed, couldn't obtain the funding when they needed it, and I'd like to be involved in some of those things. Accustaff no longer needs me other than to provide a vision. I believe the key to the success I've had is found in a lot of personal selling and building around personal relationships. Indeed, we have created an environment where by choice a large number of our personnel want to stay with us. They are challenged by new situations and opportunities as opposed to being stuck in the same job for an entire career. By the year 2000, the temporary industry will provide 5 percent of the workforce, and it's kind of fun to know that I had a part in founding that industry."

Delores was fortunate to gain her personal bearings and self-confidence as a result of a father who cared deeply about the intellectual capacity of his daughter.

▼   **Judy Singer and Patty Monteson**

> Here is a fascinating story about two entrepreneurs. Both started out as teachers, strangers to each other but sharing a desire: to leave the bureaucracy of the school system and their jobs as teachers. Judy Singer has a doctorate in education, and Patty Monteson reached the top of the pay scale in the school system in which she was teaching. Judy is an Administrator and Patty is a Tactician.

The two women ended up working for the same resort company in Pompano, Florida, and after several years of working together within the corporate structure, they decided the time had come for them to venture out on their own. Several locations and events throughout their entrepreneurial career might lead one to believe that they would never succeed. For example, they started out not knowing what business they were in because nobody had done what they were doing. When a business concept started to emerge, they hadn't a clue how to market it, and what was perhaps worse, intitially their clients really didn't understand what they were buying. Nevertheless, from the firm's shaky start in the mid-1970s to today, they are, bar none, the most successful spa consultants in the history of this country. Unlike their competition, Patty and Judy refused to believe that a spa operation inherently had to be a cash drain and a net loss for a resort operation. So in addition to designing a whole new world of spas, they turned around operations that were considered to be loss leaders. Judy explained, "I was first offered a job because people thought I could turn a spa around that had been losing money for thirteen years."

After eleven years of teaching, Judy decided the time had come for a career change. As a side business, she had been operating her own company, Health Fitness Dynamics, Inc. The firm was in the forefront of planning health, fitness, and lifestyle programs for corporations and the like. One day, she saw an advertisement in the Boston Globe for a position as director of a health spa in Florida. "I wanted to move to Florida," she said. "I applied for the job. I had no idea what a health spa was, but at least it brought me down to a warmer climate than Boston. So I quit my teaching job, sold my house, had a yard sale, and within a month moved to Florida."

The first day on the job, she attended a conference for fitness directors and there met Patty. Since 1981, the two have worked together; in Patty's words, "We worked for the company for two years, and together with the help of lots of supervisors, we turned the whole place around. The spa became a profit center and within the first year netted a million dollars in spa services."

Patty had taught school for fifteen years. She had received her master's degree in exercise psychology and commented, "A spa had never entered my mind at all. I did know, however, that I wanted to make a career change. In my school district, we took turns each year in attending a professional conference. In 1981, it was not my turn, but I felt strongly that I needed to network at this particular conference if I was going to make a change. So I quit my job and took early retirement. And now my retirement check is $103.28! So I still have to work."

The dynamics between an Administrator and a Tactician, who are determined to get along, are fascinating—even though the two of them didn't quite know what business they were in. Judy reflected on how they turned spas around: "I think that one of the early successes for us was that we were setting up systems that somehow stabilized the organization. We initiated quality control and began to set up boundaries for staff so that the guests could tell the difference between the other guests and the employees. Before we came along, they didn't know. The whole place was like 'on vacation,' and everyone was sort of doing their own thing. We began to monitor their performance and train individuals to do the job they were hired to do. We put everything in writing and began to measure performance objectively. We both became teachers again. And to tell you the truth, I think we will always be teachers, and that is why we are successful."

Patty realized that the best use of her time was to train people and enable them to do the best job they possibly could. As she explained, "In the final analysis, we set out to give guests an experience that was so satisfying that it would translate into a profitable business for the owners. While Judy oversaw the whole operation, I was very narrow in my responsibilities. All I did was to oversee the fitness department and give our guests the best value for their money. Yes, I think probably our organizational skills have become a method for following through on things and having meetings with our staffs and then follow-up." Judy adds, "Patty is also much more people oriented than I am. I have a mission. I look at the process and the steps involved while she takes care of staff, and somehow everyone wants to do the best they can for her. She knows how to soften things and get them done, while I seem to be more focused and goal oriented."

After helping turn the spa around, the time had come for the two entrepreneurs to begin to build the spa operations from an early design stage to an ongoing business. So successful were they that guests of the hotel wanted to invest in their new company. Indeed, one of their favorite clients offered to invest $25,000 in the new and unproven enterprise. They politely turned down the offer. Patty explained, "We were both flattered, but we thought the risk was too high for this person, a very successful business woman in her own right, and we didn't want to be nervous and realize that we owed somebody else. So when we started, we owned the typewriter, the business cards, and the stationery."

Patty and Judy knew they had to find a niche in a market that was ill defined. A local public relations firm assisted in publishing articles that they wrote about the spas. They also began to speak at conferences, but because the audiences were not conditioned to think creatively, Patty and Judy were viewed as people who could head up aerobics classes and provide massages for people. Nobody really understood what they were all about. Eventually, some of the more alert potential clients understood that a spa did not have to be a marketing tool and a loss leader for a resort operation. In a sense, the partners reached the concept of what they are doing today through a series of successive approximations. They began to give new information to architects, accounting firms, and interior designers and to build a blueprint that was both new and revolutionary. Remembering the initial stages, Judy explained, "During the first couple of years of our business, somebody would ask us to do something, and we said, Sure, we can do that. And then we'd run back to the office and try to figure out what 'that' was. The tools of the trade were a typewriter and a calculator. Eventually, we graduated to a computer. I also distinctly remember our first billing. It was for a well-known hotel in Bermuda. On the advice of a consultant, we were told to charge $10,000 for the job. When I announced the price to the prospective clients, they swallowed and clearly had sticker shock. So I said, Well, what is it worth to you? They said $5,000. So I said OK and that became the price. We started in an industry no one knew any thing about, and we had to go through a lot of trial and error. As we became more sophisticated, the value we contributed became more and more apparent to our clients."

As our two entrepreneurs continued on their successful path,the primary marketing and sales tools for them were the articles they wrote for resort and hotel operations and the opportunities to speak in industry-related conferences. Slowly, colleagues in the industry began to understand that spas could become highly profitable and were willing to devote more effort, time, and space to spas.

Judy and Patty explained, "Eventually our clients would come and say, 'We have profited from your input in the planning stages of the spa and we need to continue to work closely with you so that the spa will be a profit center.' And so we became more involved in operations. If you are going to build something as big as a spa, it must contribute to the bottom line. So we became as much involved in operations as we did in design. It didn't take us long to discover that no one was running the business in this industry, and there was no uniform system in accounting. They were floundering as to what message to get to the spa customers. We funded and conducted research within our own organization and researched the habits of two thousand people visiting twenty-seven spas throughout North America. So we were the first people ever to document the habits of the users and nonusers of spas."

Another reason for the success is the partners' attitude toward their clients. Intuitively, they have always known the value of going the extra mile, but in taking comprehensive responsibility for their clients, Patty explained, "Maybe we give too much value to our clients. We document everything. We give them specification books, product books, and documentation of any kind. We feel that the clients are paying for our advice, and we want to give them unbiased input. Because of this, we never receive referral fees from vendors that we recommend to supply equipment and products to our clients' spas. Unlike some of our competitors, who may submit a proposal for a lower fee than ours and then make a 'healthy' referral fee off the equipment and products they have recommended, we like to give objective, unbiased recommendations. In fact, we ask the vendors to pass on the savings to our clients so that they will get a better price. Sometimes this hurts us because we get 'low-balled' with a prospective client who is 'shopping price' and we lose the project. It is sad because, probably by the end of the project, they end up paying more because of the increased cost to them for equipment and products.

But we have learned over the years that by building a good reputation, most people who call us are doing so because they are aware of the quality of our work. We end up having a good relationship with our clients and it is also so much fun to work with them. During the past five years, there has been an appearance by other spa consultants. Instead of being threatened by them, we try to stay five steps ahead. So, when they are where we were, we are further ahead than the competition can comprehend."

During the years they have been in business, both Judy and Patty have learned to enjoy being in control of their own destiny. As Patty said, "If I cannot create something and be responsible for it, I lose something of myself, regardless of whether I succeed or fail. I think neither of us wants to fail, and we've learned to become very focused. We have been competing in a man's world, and we get calls all the time from eager developers. I think one reason we have been so successful as female entrepreneurs is because we care so deeply about the people we are privileged to work for. Our clients know our name, our reputation, and our ability to treat them with a great deal of respect. We never talk about projects we are working on, and we never put the clients on our list until the job is done. We are obsessed with doing the right thing and give them as much information as we possibly can."

Toward the end of the interview, both reflected on the kind of success they had experienced. Patty said, "If somebody speaks well of us as a company and me as an individual, I feel good about that. We have achieved what we wanted to achieve and yet our lives are somewhat out of balance. To me, real success would be to have the luxury of time, free time—which we really don't have. When we take the company to the next level, then we will be able to focus more of our energy on how we can give something back to the society that has served us so well. I think both of us would like to support individuals who want to venture out the way we did."

Judy's final comment was, "We want to start a unique company collection, which will be a gathering of our clients where we get together every year to brainstorm, talk, and share ideas in a small luxury hotel with a wonderful spa. I hope we can become a think-tank company where we can look at the trends in the business and plan and improve facilities so that they always become better. And then we can both look back and tell each other we did a good job."

CHAPTER SIX

THE IDEALIST

It is best to win
without fighting.
—Sun-Tzu

The Idealist entrepreneur more often than not enters into the entrepreneurial position unplanned. Such individuals are more accepting and in tune with changing circumstances than the other entrepreneurial types; when an opportunity emerges, an Idealist simply enters into a new realm without much questioning or reasoning. These entrepreneurs are driven by energies and forces quite different from those of the more calculating entrepreneurs.

Strategic and economic issues are not the major considerations for Idealist entrepreneurs; such issues are frequently subordinated by their desire to be with people both in the external and internal environments. They are particularly gifted in initiating and fostering long-term interpersonal relationships, endearing themselves to people throughout their career and beyond. These entrepreneurs have three unusual characteristics: (1) they are spiritual and nonmaterialistic, more oriented toward serving others than themselves; (2) they have a high capacity for subjectivity, that is, they derive a higher sense of satisfaction from bonding with people than from creating material value; and (3) they view the organization as a vehicle to accommodate people, not the other way around.

The Idealist entrepreneur's gifts are frequently neither understood nor appreciated by those who lack the ability to assume responsibility for the personal and professional growth of their employees. In this chapter, you will meet some extraordinary entrepreneurs whose success stems from their ability to understand how people are connected to one another on the interpersonal and spiritual level. Their genuine interest in people is more a matter of the heart than of the head.

Idealist entrepreneurs are masterful in creating conditions where people are inspired to deliver their very best performance. For them, hierarchies, systems, procedures, policies, and organizational efficiency take a back seat to developing a mutually supportive and productive connection with committed people. As a result of their intuitive awareness and authentic concern for people, Idealists are more easily hurt by rejection, conflict, and apathy than any of the other entrepreneurial types.

They want people to enjoy themselves in their presence. Their humanness is manifested not only in the quality of their interpersonal relationships but also in their creation of new insights, learning, and lifelong values for other people. As a matter of fact, for Idealist entrepreneurs to create value and appreciation beyond material worth and to move into the personal life-force with those they work with is a self-imposed mission, especially for introverted Idealist entrepreneurs. Psychologist Fritz Perls explained, "When my task has been accomplished, you will hardly know I was there, yet I have brought you good tidings and support nevertheless."

Modern-day management literature recommends determining vision, values, and goals through strategic planning processes, as well as managing by objectives, control, performance evaluations, and the like. Idealist entrepreneurs, however, direct their energies and attention toward the subjective and personal needs of their people. Although they may be well aware of both the traditional and conventional approaches to business, for them, establishing productive, meaningful, and mutually supportive relationships is far more important than any regimented rule or directive from the upper-echelon offices.

Idealist entrepreneurs are loving people. Their happiness comes from helping others. No wonder, then, that they do not readily fit into highly structured, impersonally organized, objectivity-driven organizations. They need the space, the freedom, and the opportunities to make their mark as mentor, friend, and motivator, helping others to stretch and reach their full potential.

When all is said and done, Idealists would be happier not relying upon rigid, disciplinary rules and formal authority to achieve their desired results. They believe that good things happen not merely because of the latest technologies but because people of their own volition and free will want to contribute to the very best of their ability. Reluctantly, however, Idealist entrepreneurs realize that systems and procedures need to be in place to accomplish goals and objectives. But their loyalty is not to infrastructures; it is to people. They are crusaders, not impersonal, controlling operators.

Because they are idealistic, they long to be an inspiration for others and to offer lifelong values in whatever endeavor they undertake—values that can never be measured in dollars and cents alone. As they strive to achieve lofty ideals, their intuition is their best and most inspiring companion. They prefer to live in a world of ideas and concepts rather than a concrete and realistic one. For them, it is far more important "to be" than "to do."

Idealist entrepreneurs tend to rely on direct interaction to communicate. Hence, they are at their best when meeting and working with people—the introverted Idealist on a one-on-one basis or in small groups, the extraverted type with larger groups—enjoying the acceptance of an audience.

Their unique capacity to establish rapport quickly is aided by their talent for understanding subtext. Thus, their communication skills are highly advanced. As one of them said, "I tend to learn more about people by watching their feet than their mouth." Being so sensitive to subtle changes, Idealists may read more into situations than is necessary. They are sensitive to nuances that deviate from proper and mutually supportive behavior. They are implicitly mindful of the notion: "I'm sure you know you thought you heard what I said. But I'm not convinced that you understand what I said was not what I intended."

Idealists use symbolic language, expressing themselves through metaphor better than most. During a recent discussion with the chairperson of a large bank, I overheard, "You, the CEO, are like the captain of the ship and you navigate according to your own judgment. Being in the chair, I represent the shipowners. I want the goods delivered on time, on location, and you figure out how to do that." For an executive, metaphor provides an opportunity to achieve a deeper understanding and communication than more prosaic language. Using symbols, the Idealist entrepreneur is able to add scope, depth, and significance.

As crusaders and prophets for enriching the value of living, Idealist entrepreneurs are always searching for authenticity. But when things go awry, they can lash out, becoming as negative as they were positive. Beware of the moment they unleash their holy wrath.

Idealists fit a different mold from the other three entrepreneurial types. When it comes down to it, however, they are viewed as substitutes or surrogates for the real thing. They must be experienced in person if they are to be understood. Capable of enjoying the material rewards of success, they are just as likely to value the simple things in life: seeing others learn and grow, listening to the wind, spending time with down-to-earth people. Nick Watry, architect, represented the essence of the Idealist when he exclaimed on a Saturday, "I can't wait till next Monday because I've got something inspirational to share with the whole staff."

Role

Idealists are frequently drafted into a leadership role they had not quite anticipated. It is the circumstances of their lives—rather than careful planning—that dictate what they end up doing. As leaders, in addition to being highly relationship and people oriented, they have a natural capacity to predict the future. They enjoy being the revealer of things to come, are fascinated by the unknown and by change.

Don't ever expect Idealist entrepreneurs to want to be in control of their subordinates or the day-to-day humdrum of concrete and rigid routines. For them, not much satisfaction comes from working within systems and procedures alone. Expect them, however, to assume all of the energy and self-control they can muster in inspiring people to perform at their very best.

Modus Operandi

Idealist entrepreneurs work best with intangibles, abstractions, and affiliations with people above and beyond the organization and its structure. Indeed, they enjoy the role of teaching and participating in both the personal and professional growth of people to whom they are close and for whom they are responsible. "Business as usual" is very boring to them. They prefer to create a set of conditions to advance their enterprise substantially beyond its current mode.

Time, for them, is perceived in long cycles: They are more interested in and dedicated to producing outstanding long-term results than being "on time." Do not expect them to be involved in formalities and procedural matters, for they want to serve, not police, their respective organizations. They prefer to work outside rather than within an organizational hierarchy. When facing an organizational chart, they are more fascinated by what's happening outside than inside the boxes that delineate the positions people hold. They know that attitudes are formulated more by process than substance and they know that the ability to influence people comes from personal qualities, energies, and commitment, not from using formal power as a crutch.

Values

Above all, Idealists value harmony. They cannot function well in high-conflict situations. Therefore, do not expect them to be particularly confrontational. Success for them comes from building the best possible human relationships. Such a humanistic orientation is often not understood and therefore not appreciated by others. In difficult and uncertain situations, Idealists rely on their faith in finding creative solutions and in obtaining results by eliciting whole-hearted performance from others as no other entrepreneurial type is able to do. They are loyal to those with whom they have elected to work as long as the relationship remains sound and supportive, and they expect reciprocity. If it is not forthcoming, they write people off.

Expectations

There is one expectation shared by every Idealist we have worked with: "I wish everyone would love me and nobody would hate me." These people cannot deliver their very best performance if others do not support one another and function like members of extended families. They have a high need to be accepted, supported, and at times admired by their co-workers and the greater community. They love to shine, to charm people by reaching out to them, and are particularly insightful about people and their motivation. They listen intensely to their own inner voice, relying heavily on intuition and deep-seated personal values, ultimately determining their attitude and appropriate expectations for each person on an individual basis.

Idealists are fascinated by events and situations that help them to gain insights. Typically, they enjoy demonstrating their deep understanding of people and complex situations before anyone else can. When people disagree, critique, and refuse to show empathy, Idealists are likely to withdraw, hurt. They stay inside their shells as long as they perceive they are not receiving the support they so richly deserve. They may stew over problems and their consequences for days and weeks, in order to arrive at a conclusion they can live with. Their tendency is to eliminate pain by moving elsewhere or assuring that those who can potentially hurt them are moved elsewhere. But if they feel an injustice has been done, they can lash out vehemently with anger, frustration, and disappointment.

To the uninformed, the Idealist may appear wishy-washy, weak, demonstrating a lack of capacity to deal with conflict. However, Idealists rarely undertake significant changes without considering their innermost values and beliefs. Without flinching and without compromise, these entrepreneurs are able to do what has to be done, even if their action results in disappointment and pain. This behavior is why particularly introverted Idealist types may seem mystical and secretive.

Lifestyle

When Idealist entrepreneurs wake up in the morning, their inner, beautifully colored achievement display screen is not only full but overloaded with great intentions and great expectations. There aren't enough hours in the day for them. They prefer to allocate an inordinate amount of time to people they personally find fascinating, sometimes at the cost of optimizing the performance of their business. For them, nothing is more important than devoting time to those they serve—and indeed their leadership style is one of serving; their philosophy is "I must let my people lead me, for I am their leader." Idealists surf through life, picking up on the smallest cues in the environment around them, devoting themselves to others and especially to their own families. But there are times when the demands of the business will cause them to jeopardize both their personal and family life.

In daily life, Idealists are loaded with things to do, sometimes at the cost of "what to be." Their inner drive to live up to a set of idealistic goals and objectives is sometimes not realistic. Their need to inspire and their humbleness, kindness, and supportiveness both within and outside their environment can become an encumbrance.

▼ Nick Watry, CEO of Watry Design

Nick Watry, the oldest of three children, was born in Oakland, California, and grew up in Merced. At the time of his birth, he became somewhat physically handicapped and throughout his life has been acutely aware of his limitations. When he was twelve years old, his father went into bankruptcy and his parents divorced.

Nick is the Idealist entrepreneur personified and throughout his life has been an energetic high achiever. He is a born leader, motivated by being an inspiration to people and outperforming his handicap any way he can. He has a zest for life and will never really grow old because he is constantly exploring new ideas and concepts; currently, he is working on his master's degree in architecture. Much like Andre Staffelbach, he grew up with a pencil in his hand. Unlike Andre, Nick is extremely auditory whereas Andre is highly visual. Nick describes himself: "I'm a handicapped person with a wounded right wing. I think that has a lot to do with the fact that I feel triply privileged to be here. After I got past the health and injury problems,

I recall a very happy life full of fantasy until I was twelve, when my parents divorced. I spent a lot of time listening to the radio, and from as far back as I can remember I sketched boats, clowns, and caricatures that I saw literally and imagined around me. I had a lot of fun learning. I was handicapped throughout my formative years, and I never learned to read nor write to the class level I was in. I had an IQ of 137, and I was always ridiculed about not reaching my potential. I remember those years as ones of being placed in the back of the class because I was behind. The teachers didn't have much to do with me. Again, looking out the windows fantasizing and daydreaming about the future caused me to get further and further behind in school. Those years impacted the way I am today, and it has something to do with my self-image. I knew I was a minority character."

Compensating for these handicaps, Nick seemed to derive exceptional energy from his involvement with extracurricular activities, and in his early teens he participated in youth groups, clubs, and volunteer activities. Moreover, his mother, who did not remarry, made it clear to Nick that he was the man of the house. He explained, "Taking on that responsibility gave me a sense of significance and importance that I might not otherwise have had. I was capable and successful at it. I think it prepared me for what I'm doing now, being responsible for both my firm and the people working in it."

When Nick was about fifteen years old he learned how to play the drums and became very good at it. He joined a high school precision band that was honored statewide. "In those days, in the fifties, those in the band all had the same classes together, and it was natural for us to go on to college. None of my family had ever gone to college, and conversations at home were never about what you were going to do when you grew up. I was definitely pulled along by my peer group. I thank them. I began to break away and became very strong and deliberate when I went to college. My mother, probably to this day, is very upset with that because I found the outside world more stimulating, adventuresome, and exciting than going home to a small town. I played in the band for four years and went on many trips. People liked me a lot, and I was very much trusted—in church, in school, and in the family. I was looked upon as a leader because I listened in my leadership role."

Toward the end of college, Nick did volunteer work for the Episcopal Church and for a well-known bishop at that time, James Pike: "He was a very powerful, mystical man in my life. One day when I was nineteen I said to him, 'Bishop Pike, I have a question for you. Should I be an Episcopalian priest or an architect?' Without hesitation, the bishop answered, 'You should be an architect because you can better serve humanity as an architect than as a priest. That's who you are.' And so I said, 'Yeah, that's who I am.'"

Nick's work ethic is exceptional. "Ever since I was eleven years old, I loved work because it defined me better. It allowed me to be with people who were exciting and interesting, be it a professor, a customer or a colleague. I feel blessed that I wake up in the morning and go and do exactly what I want to do. I'm pulled into architecture and engineering and I love what it's all about."

Nick did not set out in life to become an entrepreneur. Upon receiving his architectural degree at the age of twenty-two, he went to work in Honolulu, in the prestressed concrete post tension segment of the construction industry. Within six months, he helped build an organization employing 180 people. But in spite of his success in Hawaii, Nick wanted to return to San Francisco and assume a lower-level position in the firm. Times were tough, and the oil embargo caused construction to plummet. In his inimitable Idealist style, Nick felt he was overpaid and was not contributing enough value, so he quit. "To be an entrepreneur was never an internal motivation or goal. I started modestly in 1975 and never wanted to, nor expected to, do anything other than just make a modest living, and do the fun things I liked to do. So now, twenty years later, the Watry Design business has grown from annual revenues of $120,000 to presently achieving revenues in excess of $2 million. All of that happened because people hired me to do what I liked doing and supported me in growing the business. I did not, however, have a business plan, nor do I have one today."

Nick's motivation for being an entrepreneur is, to say the least, different from that of the majority of self-made people. There is both a spirit and a spirituality in what Nick does. His ambition is to provide value both for customers and for people in his own organization. When he was asked what are the trivialities in his work, somewhat to our surprise he answered, "The necessity of money to run the day-to-day operation and invest in the future—I'm definitely not money oriented, profit driven, and materialistic. These considerations spoil the joy of work. Fortunately, we have other people here who watch over that end of the store. I'm up at the front window creating the attractive display that brings in the customers, probably even doing a jig or a dance, then I run behind the counter and serve."

Not surprisingly, Nick has little use for organizational hierarchies, titles, and internal politics. He is far more interested in the individuals themselves, and he talks about how people seldom leave his company, how they become highly valued contributors in the design work. David LoCoco, for example, joined Nick when he was nineteen years old and has been instrumental in evolving micro-systems and training people in the art of designing prestressed concrete building structures such as parking garages and hotels. One of Nick's great strengths is his appreciation and recognition of people, and he said, "David brought to the firm something that absolutely I could not do myself, but I saw his potential and he didn't. I was able to support him emotionally and financially. Today he is probably one of the foremost [computer-aided] designers in America. He can't do what I do and I can't do what he does."

In keeping with his somewhat unorthodox method of running a business, Nick does not place much value on people advancing into managerial positions. In his opinion, values are created not by organizational structures but by people doing their jobs. "Those in senior positions have to earn it, and they have to earn it in their view and not mine, and then they have to ask for it. I don't feel I'm the one to anoint anybody. I have difficulty going to someone because I need them to be in upper management. In this firm, people in high positions are not compensated as well as some of our best engineers. Perhaps that's why most of the people working with me never leave. Take Michelle, for example. She became my soulmate in design. We could communicate without talking. There was neither any conflict nor waste of time. Some of our best work has come from the two of us working together."

Nick is polyactive, and despite his work with prestressed concrete, he knows nothing about personal stress. In addition to managing his business, he is a planning commissioner in Redwood City, president of the American Concrete Institute, and a full-time graduate student working on a thesis that may cause radical changes in how buildings are constructed in earthquake zones. "I'm an inventor and I have designed and built over 680 buildings. Half of them I have never seen. I love to solve the problems and work out the direction that affects other people's lives, but I don't need to see their lives affected. It is the process that I love so much, not the glory of the consequences."

When he was asked what he would have done differently, Nick said, "Save money. I was born to borrow, born to spend. I have an immense faith in the future that big money will be there. This never comes to the level expected. I'm continuously criticized for overpaying employees, including their bonuses. I do not go cheap. I buy the best paper, the best computers, the best space—even if I can't afford it. I do not cut coupons and I do not go to sales. I overtip and overpay, because I think people are worth it and I'm worth it. I should be overpaid."

Clearly, Nick's approach to running a business is somewhat out of the ordinary. Keep in mind, however, that as an Idealist entrepreneur, Nick is nonmaterialistic; the satisfaction he derives from just being there and working with people overshadows the profit motivation. He loves life for what it is, not what it *could* be. "I know I am a high risktaker. Sometimes I hit and sometimes I miss. I wish I could have partners, but no one wants to partner with me because I am not focused on money, and I know I'm the butt of the jokes in the family. My brother said, 'You're the most successful Watry. You made it in spite of yourself.' The bottom line is I made it because I love what I do and thank goodness that this country, this environment, this business, pays people for the excellence of their talents and gifts."

Nick Watry will never grow up: His capacity to live life for all it's worth makes him a unique, happy entrepreneur. It is natural for him to walk a fine line between making money and finding fulfillment. "The satisfaction I derive from being an entrepreneur is to know I made a difference. To have a business that designs things which will last well beyond my presence and to live within one's own creation is all I could ask for. A typical worker in the United States works 100,000 hours in a lifetime. When I was fifty-two, I calculated that I had worked 160,000 hours. If my work were not my life, I would never have done that. I feel so liberated as a person to know that I have something of value and importance to give to the rest of the population. One of my clients said it all when he suggested, 'Nick is unbelievably insightful in understanding where people are coming from. I would find it hard to work with any other design group after the Nick experience.'"

No doubt Nick has often forfeited the opportunity to maximize profits. But he has been able to maximize his life both personally and professionally, and that is more valuable to him than money. At the end of his working days, Nick may not leave a large fortune behind, but he will leave a legend larger than life.

▼ Rick Vidgen, CEO of MacFarms

Rick Vidgen was born and raised in Queensland, Australia. Before he was born, his father joined the Australian Army and was given up as lost in action during the Second World War. It turned out that he was detained in a Japanese concentration camp, and he returned to Australia when Rick was five years old. The significance of these events are etched in Rick's life: "My father came back an old man even though he survived. He wouldn't talk much and he had somewhat of an existential philosophy that got him through the war living on nothing. I do not have many particularly pleasant memories of my childhood except when I was with my grandparents whom I adored. So at a young age I knew the sooner I could be independent the better. Breaking away from the family was easy. I never expected to get anything from my family—not that they ever had a whole heap of money. I always felt that they gave me an education and that was all I ever deserved. I wanted to work as soon as I could because it would give me money and I could be more independent."

Rick's particular circumstances shaped his expectations differently from the typical American entrepreneur. Also, he grew up in a more relaxed culture than the highly competitive American environment. He entered into his productive life through the Australian back door before coming through the American front door to be the CEO of the largest macadamia nut company in the world.

Rick is a relatively complex person. He is intimate, comfortable when he works with few people, and not especially gregarious. A quiet individual, he is not likely to flair up or display great moments of enthusiasm. If anything, he is more reflective than active. When he works with people, it is very easy for him to express himself, for he has an insatiable need for information and involvement. He is far more visual than he is auditory, and what he can see sticks with him better than what he hears. His introversion reflects a need for privacy, seclusion, and quietly and harmoniously dealing with the issues of the day, but he is warm toward others.

As an Idealist entrepreneur, it is difficult for Rick to deal with the day-to-day routines in his organization; he is more comfortable with ideas and abstractions. He enjoys intellectual pursuits and can spend much time philosophizing and searching for the purpose and meaning of just about anything. Much of his success at MacFarms can be attributed to the fact that for him nothing is ever good enough; he perpetually searches for new ways to add value to MacFarms. In addition, Rick is a realistic individual and therefore has the capacity to translate entrepreneurial dreams into realities. For example, one of the major thoughts guiding his actions is to move the macadamia nuts industry away from the commodity market to become a product perceived to have much higher value than the competition.

A compassionate man, Rick prefers the affective to the logical realm. He has a deep respect and love for people, and, in his present situation, he has much concern for the livelihood of his company's 250 employees on the big island in Hawaii. Sometimes people are threatened by his tendency to constantly question, but his intent is only to gain more knowledge so he can make better decisions.

Like so many other entrepreneurs, Rick is polyactive and derives energy from doing many things simultaneously. He is exceptionally open for change and can cope with crisis situations better than most. Over the past few years, he has gone to great lengths in planning for the growth of his firm. Yet he is very aware of the fact that he is aiming at a moving target, and his readiness for change has provided the firm with substantial advantages. Although not a born entrepreneur, he is a born leader who moves steadily toward the goals he sets for himself and he is always decisive. Yet he is aware of the fact that because of his willingness to be open to new input, he all too easily becomes distracted from what he set out to do. He said, "Anything that gets a little boring I just don't do well at."

Rick's early career was with a large Australian food-producing corporation where he was on a fast track to become one of the top executives. After twenty-four years with the company, he realized that he was not achieving what he really wanted in his life. "I originally signed up because I thought it was a way of being independent and working with a team of people who were real winners. I stayed with them far too long, and I realized that I got to a point where I had to share values with people who lacked my sense of ethical standards. It was time to get out, and unfortunately I found that out much later than I should have. I suddenly discovered that I really disliked the corporate world even though I had advanced rapidly up the corporate ladder. I loved the idea of sitting down with people and helping them organize a better life for themselves. I know I did a lot of good things because people trusted me. I also found out that the top executives in the firm didn't work as hard as I did, and when I looked at their lifestyles, I didn't like the situation. So I began to realize that people who stayed on in corporations became part of a value structure I didn't want. In order to continue to progress I had to compromise my ethics, and suddenly I realized that I don't like these people because they tell lies and cheat and I knew that this was not right."

Rick has been the CEO of MacFarms since 1990, and during that period he has upgraded the firm from being in a net loss position to becoming highly profitable. In reflecting on his success, he explained, "I really was master of my own destiny. I began to understand that what was important to me wasn't the acquisition of large amounts of money or large amounts of power. Rather, it was to serve in an organization with the potential to really make a difference."

In the process of turning the firm around, Rick worked on a one-on-one basis with his key managers. "The best employees we have, I believe, are the people who are fitted into the right job slot and who are encouraged to operate within their capabilities. I also believe you have to give people the right tools to be successful. Because we put so much value on each individual, our organizational form is unimportant. That is why we've been able to hold on to the best salesperson in the industry. We have an excellent factory manager, and he is being stretched all of the time to come up with new technologies, which he has done successfully. We have an orchard manager who lives and breathes for the orchard. When it doesn't rain, it becomes a personal problem for him. It all comes back to the basic truth that if you genuinely care for people and let them do what they are good at, they, and ultimately MacFarms, have to be successful."

So relatively late in life Rick discovered and took responsibility for the fact that he was, as he said, the master of his own destiny. He brought with him to MacFarms experience, patience, and wisdom, and by departing from what for him were dysfunctional, large corporate values, he got back in touch with who he really is as a person. If we were to visit with Rick today, we would find him deeply involved in his community. He told us, "We are building a new school. For me, making that school successful is enormously important. We have acquired the land and the community is working together to create the best learning environment we can for our children. I'm also deeply committed to the Nutrition Project because I believe the future of the whole nut industry is a vital link for people to be healthy. I like to make things work and I'm not all that interested in the details afterwards. In my younger years, I wanted recognition. I have discovered that it means very little. There are always a lot of people clapping because they feel they should. What is important is that with a team we have moved mountains. I've learned to no longer seek praise from above and flattery from below."

Rick's success has always carried a price, and, he is willing to pay that price. He said, "In my view, if you're going to be successful, you've got to really want to be successful. If you don't you will have to accept second best, and for me that doesn't work."

True to his Idealist style, Rick enjoys his family. "I don't take vacations because I travel too much anyway. I have a very nice house, and I like to have friends around or just the family and enjoy them and quiet times."

▼ Barbara Edwards, CEO of California Host

When Barbara was nine years old, her father's entrepreneurial venture failed and he filed for bankruptcy. Abruptly, the good life in the suburbs vanished and was replaced with an urban existence. Barbara explained, "This put a lot of responsibility on me and my brother. My father would come home from work at 4 in the afternoon and my mom had just left to go to her job. Every day, I had to come straight home from school and take care of my younger brother. Up until I was about seventeen years old, I had a lot of responsibility, cooking, laundering, managing, and doing whatever it took." Barbara's company, California Host, has just celebrated its twenty-fifth anniversary. California Host serves as a public relations firm and major event coordinator for corporate clients such as Apple and Hewlett-Packard. Her company specializes in orchestrating all the logistics of important event planning, from the booking of hotels and limosines to the selection of enter-tainment, menus, and invitations. The meetings have spanned twenty-six countries and have included the special treatment needed for foreign heads of state and dignitaries such as the Pope.

During these difficult years, Barbara also discovered her expectations and lifestyle were quite different from those of her parents, and at a young age she became independent and highly self-reliant. She explained, "I felt I didn't match my parents in much of anything. Their beliefs, values, and principles were so different from mine. My father used to say 'All your ideas are out of this world.' I have a much greater intellectual span than my parents ever did and I used to think they were sitting in a box while I was breaking the barriers. At that time, I decided I wasn't going to cause my parents any more prob-lems. I was going to make their lives easier. From the time I was twelve years old, I bought everything I needed with my own money. I was very ambitious. I could handle two or three jobs at the same time. My parents knew I had a lot of power, and they also knew I was responsible. I think I was a good daughter. I never caused any problems. I had a real sense of justice, and I knew what was right and what was wrong. In school I got involved in everything, and I loved to plan activities and events. In fact, I realized I just made things happen. It was as easy for me then as it is today to translate ideas into action."

During this period, Barbara spent a fair amount of time with her favorite aunt, who molded the kind of lifestyle Barbara wanted for herself. She discovered that her aunt placed a high premium on hon-esty, open communication, cooperation, and solid team member-ship—characteristics that became the foundation for Barbara's suc-cess. She explained, "We all have to be part of a team, yet we have to honor diversity, and sometimes people who are not natural team players have a better individual vision and understanding of what needs to be done. What I've learned is not to direct my business to-ward competition but to do the very, very best we can by providing the highest performance possible, while giving our customers our total soul and full capacity. My tendency is to look at the big picture even though I can be good with details. But I don't like the repetitive and the mundane. Therefore, I've surrounded myself with a staff that complements my intuition. One of today's idioms is the notion of empowerment. That's OK, but I have learned if I don't have enough confidence in people, I cannot possibly give them the responsibility they need to get the job done. Because I came from the school of hard knocks, I have a special affection for our middle management. They are willing to do almost anything. And sometimes they bite off much more than they can chew."

Despite Barbara's unusual capacity to be a mover and a shaker in the hospitality industry, the sailing was not always smooth. During a high growth period, her husband, who was a professor, barred her from reaching out and building the business as fast as she thought she could. She commented, "Every time I wanted to expand my business my husband became very insecure and would say, 'No, no, your business is perfect. Leave it the way it is. Why do you always have to take these big chances?' He'd put a harness on me during the time when Silicon Valley was growing up. I had to break the mold with companies such as Apple Computer, Intel, National Semiconductor, Hewlett-Packard, and IBM. Each of the aforementioned companies became large clients. In the final analysis, I did what I wanted to do. I worked with Steven Jobs and John Scully over at Apple. I worked with both Mr. Hewlett and Mr. Packard and I took advantage of the opportunities to provide these companies with services no competitor could match. Throughout our whole organization, there was both a commitment and willingness to get the job done."

Barbara has learned to live with frustration and ambiguity, perhaps more so than most entrepreneurs. Her clients typically change their minds several times at the last minute and everything that has been put together has to be redesigned and re-engineered. She has learned, "If we are not flexible, we cannot achieve the best results for our clients, simply because there are so many cooks in the kitchen. There are only a couple of clients I decided I could not work with. Their indecisiveness made it impossible for us to perform. To succeed, you have to be proactive but you must have enough time to implement changing ideas."

Barbara is an idea-per-minute person in addition to taking care of the day-to-day work in her hospitality business. She explained, "At any moment, I could probably think of five companies I would like to start. Yet I'm realistic enough to know that I have neither the energy nor the people resources to succeed as a multiple entrepreneur. I'm a hands-on manager, and I'm obsessed with always delivering the highest possible quality. I get into it 100 percent. Mind you, I have lots of failures, but I learn from them. You pick yourself back up, you do it a different way, you correct errors, and you learn. Failure doesn't scare me, recovery does."

It was through her success pattern that the organization took on a life of its own. Over the last ten years, her company has enjoyed a compounded annual growth rate of roughly 30 percent until the recession hit. When the demand for hospitality services disappeared for a period of time, she explained, "I don't think I had the foresight to understand a recession at the time we went from sixteen to four employees. Had I not put $250,000 of my own money into the company, we would have become history. I knew it was the right thing to do. By now I've been paid back my money, and I've learned to be much more cautious."

Yet Barbara refuses to impose limitations upon her creativity. "We have a lot of landmarks, and one of the most exciting assignments was to be part of announcing new products for Microsoft. All of a sudden, I received a phone call from a client who worked with another company five years ago, and they told me, 'I want to use you again because I know you're the only one who can get the job done.' That trust and loyalty means more to me than all the landmark opportunities put together. I've worked for more than twenty-four years with Hewlett-Packard and Apple and still have a relationship with them that no one else can beat."

In trying to explain the basic reasons for her phenomenal success, she said, "I was raised to please people, and I think that's why I may be successful in my business. I think the higher power looked down, and the gift that was bestowed upon me as an individual was to create forums for large groups of people to come together and experience moments of happiness and satisfaction they never forget. I hope that I have fulfilled that. Given all the things that have happened to me, I've had a very, very good life, albeit tough at times. The only problem I experience at this stage is that I put all of my time and energy into my work and I have no personal life. My tendency is to put myself in the back seat and to put everyone else in front of me. I'm driven to always improve on my success and be financially independent."

Barbara has a huge imagination. She deals with abstractions with a flair few can match, shies away from tradition, and admires originality. More auditory than visual, she has the ability to listen to what people mean, not necessarily what they say. Another of her great strengths is that she is both questioning and accepting. She asks questions in order to learn and gain a deeper understanding of her client's needs and, because she is so accepting, never criticizes from a negative point of view. The nature of her work is guided by an affective domain. Implicitly, she knows that recognizing the emotional components in the events she creates is more important than taking a purely rational approach.

Barbara can operate at multiple levels and take on a number of assignments simultaneously without becoming confused or frustrated. There is a spontaneity in everything she does, which allows her to respond to clients' needs in an unobtrusive and positive fashion. Yet she is a great planner and believes that planning is necessary to achieve quality results. Furthermore, she is an optimist who worries cautiously. In other words, she has great faith that the events she creates will turn out to be positive as long as she is mindful that things can go wrong. When a decision needs to be made, she will make it, and when all the facts and figures are in she naturally assumes leadership. "Our company is a leading company as a result of our reputation. I know that sometimes I come across as arrogant and I'm really not. For some reason, I have the capacity to see what will happen in the future, and by intuition I know if we are on a collision course. I believe we are one of the two leading companies in our discipline."

Barbara realizes that because she is a hands-on person, involved in day-to-day operations, she may not have built the proper infrastructure. During the final moments of our conversation, she explained, "I think I might have done things differently if I had had a mentor, someone I could have learned from so that I could have saved myself from mistakes. I created California Host without a model and without really knowing what I was doing because there were no role models. Not only did I have to learn along the way, I'm also in an industry dominated by men. It was difficult to break the mold. I didn't let that stop me."

CHAPTER SEVEN

PARTNERS IN SUCCESS

What man has not yet done
is only what he has not yet
attempted to do.
—Alexis de Tocqueville

I n this chapter, we will discuss how you as an entrepreneur can begin to think about the type of people who are your best complements in achieving and sustaining success, because chances are you can't do it all by yourself.

Assume for a moment that you are an Administrator type of entrepreneur. Just as birds of a feather flock together, you are likely to derive satisfaction and comfort from working with no-nonsense people like yourself. The problem is, similarity and familiarity do not necessarily produce the results you need for your organization to lead the pack. Successful entrepreneurs implicitly understand the need to work with people of different and complementary styles. Indeed, entrepreneurs who honor diversity will always have a leg up on the competition; if they are capable of identifying and attracting individuals who possess the unique skills and the experience required for growth—and are willing to leave their personal comfort zone out of the equation—they will be less susceptible to stagnation and advantageously positioned for adapting to changing times and swiftly shifting markets.

All too often, successful people focus on their shortcomings and resolve to become better performers in areas of weakness and even disinterest, in order to achieve better results. But I have yet to see an entrepreneur enjoying great success by dwelling upon his or her weaknesses. In fact, entrepreneurial organizations that build and sustain success are made up of people who are encouraged to be who they are and to do what they do best. Therefore, if the organizational philosophy is to create an environment where each person is encouraged and supported in doing what he or she does best, the total human synergy is likely to allow the entrepreneur to lift the individual, along with the organization, by the same tide.

If, for example, you are an Administrator or a Tactician, what are you good at? Operations. You are best at hands-on and concrete tasks. You derive satisfaction from doing things and seeing results, not contemplating and theorizing. As a Tactician, you want to have your hand in as many results as possible in order to derive a sense of personal satisfaction from making your best contribution. Granted, as an Administrator, you may be somewhat less hands-on than the Tactician entrepreneur, yet you are at your best when you focus on meeting and exceeding expectations by personally being involved in the day-to-day activities of the organization.

If, on the other hand, you are a Strategist, you tend to be more abstract, using your imagination and foresight to contemplate the future. Attracting other Strategic types to work with you can be quite stimulating. The problem, however, may be that whereas the work environment is intensely stimulating, the day-to-day stuff is neglected.

This is not to suggest that you hire people according to their brand of entrepreneurial style—there is more to work life than people's styles. Who people are is a result of complexities well beyond the notion of styles; it has to do with circumstances at birth, expectations, and emotional stability developed as a reflection of inherent values, maturity, and other influences. Nevertheless, when you are interviewing people for key positions, knowing their entrepreneurial style will give you an edge in understanding how they are likely to operate. That alone, however, is not sufficient for establishing long-term productive relationships. Other aspects, such as cultural differences, personal dictates, and especially shared values and self-motivation, have a decisive impact on how people are likely to perform.

Assuming you have an idea of what your entrepreneurial style is, let's see how others may complement you. Naturally, if you are like hundreds of other entrepreneurs, you probably have a fairly healthy ego and a desire for outstanding accomplishment. Without a strong ego, you would not have become a high achiever. However, letting your ego stand in the way of allowing others to do what they do best is counterproductive.

Your personal growth inevitably will include an understanding of and an appreciation for the diverse gifts of other people. As you age, you will become wiser and more capable of working and living with people who affect you in unexpected ways. It follows that your entrepreneurial journey can be immensely altered by those with whom you choose to work. John Dean, the eminently successful CEO of Silicon Valley Bank, said, "You know, I can't even start thinking about work until I have my team assembled and ready to go." It took John almost a year to identify the ten key players needed to start and accelerate the journey that has led the bank to unparalleled success in the financial industry.

The Administrator

As an Administrator entrepreneur, your personal and professional life is one of deep devotion and an ingrained sense of duty to those you serve and with whom you work. You believe in hard, smart work. You are driven by a sense of owing people, providing for them, and, above all, being the responsible overseer. In order to understand how Tactician, Strategist, and Idealist types complement your style, you might find the following contrasts and comparisons useful.

Your Role Perception

In your work situation, you strongly emphasize dependability, responsibility, and a team spirit. In your day-to-day work, you prefer competent co-workers and require predictability, order, systems, and established procedures. You encourage delegation of authority and responsibility. Job descriptions are also appropriate so people know what is expected of them, eventually allowing for an evaluation of their performance. You derive a sense of inner peace when things are stable and operating according to plan. You tend to be both top- and bottom-line oriented, knowing that the economics of your work situation is the lifeblood of your organization. You do not respond well to impulse.

You are not a futurist because you are anchored in the certainty of the past. You tend to be linear in your approach: There is a beginning, an orderly process for progress, and a natural or logical conclusion. You are a cautious risktaker. If you are an introverted Administrator, you may become bogged down in details and micromanagement. If everything works according to budgets and plans and your expectations and standards are met, life is good. You avoid crisis management at all costs.

As a responsible entrepreneur, you naturally worry a great deal; if you are not worried, you may be very worried about the fact that there is nothing to worry about. Finally, you tend to be ceremonial in your approach; the tried and true are your anchors. Anything promoted as revolutionary, brand-new, and incredibly fantastic turns you off. Now let's look at complementary styles.

The Complementary Role of the Tactician

Perhaps the most difficult co-worker for you is the Tactician. At several levels, the Tactician is your exact opposite, being not especially disciplined and with little or no use for hierarchies, predictabilities, and systematic approaches. Nonetheless, Tacticians have a real knack for sizing up opportunities at critical moments. The problem is, of course, that they tend to be risktakers, and you may suffer the consequences. Tacticians enjoy life in the fast lane but can slam on the brakes suddenly while accelerating. Tacticians "live and let live," savoring every moment. Their orientation is to the here and now, and they trust their impulses more than thoughtful calculations and careful appraisals of situations. So you need Tacticians to produce positive results as long as you calculate the risks.

You need to know that because Tacticians are extremely situational, they need to make the kind of impact that provides the feedback reward they are looking for. Also, know that your Tactician complements generally do not operate at the conceptual level; rather, they are highly operational and will appreciate you if you are uncompromising in producing superb quality. Tacticians can charm their way through all kinds of obstacles and are masterful in turning threats into opportunities, negatives into positives, and marginal returns into successes. When unpleasant surprises occur, Administrators are usually angry and frustrated to the point of paralysis, whereas Tacticians sense unseen opportunities and use their great negotiating skills.

As an Administrator, you work at work, and if time allows, you enjoy playing at play. Your Tactician counterpart, however, enjoys playing at play but is also inclined to play at work. Whereas you tend to be stern, goal oriented, and serious, your Tactical colleague is light-hearted, taking nothing very seriously. You feel that you must earn the right to progress; because things do not fall into your lap, you are prepared to work hard, then at some future point enjoy the fruits of your labor. The Tactician, however, wants instant gratification and insists upon enjoying the good life now before it's too late. Thus your Tactician complement provides awareness of immediate advantages, in contrast to your anticipated and orderly performance.

Be aware, though, that Tacticians are difficult to manage and are not really team players. They perform best in crisis situations and are masterful troubleshooters but need space to respond to their own priorities.

In summary, your Tactician complement can take advantage of circumstances not emanating from predictable situations and careful anticipation, providing value when things are confusing, uncertain, and out of balance. Tacticians shine when you may be at a loss for what to do.

The Complementary Role of the Strategist

The most valuable complement for you as an Administrator entrepreneur may be the Strategist entrepreneur. The reason is simple: You have a great capacity to deal realistically and concretely with issues and to get things done, while the Strategist complements you by being abstract and conceptual, raising issues often critical for the future. Much of your life is focused on the present whereas Strategists push the boundaries and move into the future elegantly and effortlessly.

Strategists have a high capacity to identify opportunities that have not necessarily been fully defined, and they have little or no time for the here and now. Actually, they can turn out to be intellectual dilettantes, arrogant, and out of touch with your realities.

Whereas you are constantly burdened by responsibility and duty, the Strategist has an insatiable need to access more knowledge and become more competent in focused areas of endeavor. Your approach is linear, whereas Strategists roam, so to speak, trying to understand how all the pieces fit together to allow your organization to move ahead of your competitors.

Consider a Strategist to be potentially a great long-term complement for you, albeit at times operating at levels you may neither fully understand nor appreciate in the short haul. When the chips are down, the Strategist entrepreneur, although a loner, can help you comprehend how to create conditions today that will benefit the organization tomorrow.

The Complementary Role of the Idealist

You have one thing in common with an Idealist colleague: You are both strong team players. While your loyalties go to the economics and the growth side of the organization, Idealist entrepreneurs' loyalties go to the spirit and the soul of the people with whom they are working, an attitude you may not readily understand but which eventually you may accept. Idealists have the unique gift and capability for working with people from the inside out, trying to understand them, whereas others are trying to be understood.

As an Administrator, you expect people to perform, but Idealists tend to inspire them to do their best. Idealists focus on how people in an organization can realize their potential. They have big hearts and can use diplomacy to elicit the best from people, so do not be surprised if your Idealist counterpart brings out the best both in yourself and your team in determining where you want to take your organization. Superb facilitators, they involve themselves both intellectually and emotionally to bring your enterprise to peak performance.

Idealists also use symbolic language to take the most complex concepts and convert and simplify them into easily understood mental impressions.

As a realistic Administrator entrepreneur, you may not be particularly imaginative, but your Idealist counterpart can dream and envision the future. However, in order to absorb impressions from a wide variety of sources, the Idealist may be overly gullible at times and lack critical capability, or may even be too idealistic given the realities of your enterprise.

Idealists tend to invest all they have—mental capacity, affection, energy—in their organization. Thus they can feel rejected and hurt if they are left out. Sometimes they burn out in their zeal to be the collective conscience and soulmate of everyone they work with.

Idealists are also especially gifted in processing data and reaching functional decisions from an inspirational and subjective perspective that is much different from yours and that otherwise may not be available for you. This could potentially improve your decision-making process dramatically.

The Tactician

If you are a Tactician entrepreneur, what you bring to any situation is perhaps the highest instinct for survival of all entrepreneurs together with an ability to handle unforeseen surprises and crisis situations with more flair and elegance than the others. Once you have a comprehensive view of what kind of entrepreneur you want to be, very little, if anything, can hold you back. Be mindful of the fact, however, that sometimes you tend to be a risktaker to a degree that may be detrimental to your financial and even your personal health. However, as an entrepreneur, failure is not in your vocabulary. If things go astray or don't click, you view them as merely temporary setbacks.

Your Role Perception

You tend to be exceptionally alert to new opportunities, more from a tactical than a strategic point of view. You don't sit back and contemplate; rather, you are in the thick of things, eminently capable of taking advantage of a specific situation to practice your entrepreneurial capabilities. You are exceptionally skilled in maneuvering in uncharted waters and pulling together a group of people to get things done, especially in difficult times. Indeed, you enjoy the challenge of coping with the unknown and bringing to bear whatever it takes to make things go well. People want to follow you because you are charismatic, you exude expertise, self-confidence, and a healthy respect for your clients and customers.

As an entrepreneur, you do not dwell on theories and conceptual frameworks, nor are you likely to be found in your office a great deal—you need to be where the action is. Quickly and accurately, you give people their marching orders and see that it all comes together. You are fiercely independent, provide people with the information they need at the moment, and enjoy challenging your workers to deliver their best performance. You know no boundaries in terms of what people are capable of doing. Hence, you have high expectations for yourself and your fellow leaders in the firm.

The Complementary Role of the Administrator

Although you share the sensing capability with the Administrator, an Administrator type can be of significant value for you. You focus your energies where you see the highest need. You believe that people should be smart enough to figure out what needs to be done, and if everybody pitches in and does their job, management, structure, and bureaucracy is wasteful and nonproductive overhead. The best contribution an Administrator can make is to assist in the structural work of building an organization, a task that at times feels like an albatross around your neck.

Do not expect that working along with an Administrator is going to be easy. True, you are both realistic, but your realism is directed toward different kinds of performance. As a Tactician, your spontaneity and awareness of what needs to be done from moment to moment are not necessarily in sync with the Administrator, who is more concerned with building an infrastructure that will perpetuate and sustain itself. Do not be upset when you find it difficult to recognize the value provided by your Administrator partner. Realize that you tend to be a rugged individualist whereas an Administrator is more conservative, places more trust in a team effort, and thereby provides leverage and a more effective and efficient working environment.

Like you, an Administrator is operationally inclined and not particularly conceptual. Unlike you, however, an Administrator likes to bring order out of chaos and establish standards for performance through specific routines and work methodologies. You, as a Tactician entrepreneur, are at your best when things are confused and your skills and gifts are needed; the Administrator derives satisfaction from making things work according to plan.

Your Administrator partner can also be a significant complement because you tend to be a great promoter, whereas the Administrator tends toward providing direction for an organization to become highly efficient. In fact, the Administrator is obsessed with efficiency and doing things right but does not always perform effectively or do the right things. Nevertheless, an Administrator manager can be an ideal complement in striving for your enterprise to deliver products and services responsibly and according to plans, commitments, and expectations.

The Complementary Role of a Strategist

Although the orientation of a Strategist is vastly different from that of a Tactician, under the right set of circumstances a Strategist may be the most valuable human asset for you. Your exact opposite, the Strategist brings conceptual abilities to the organization.

Highly achievement oriented, he or she, like you, tends to approach work in an individualistic rather than a team-focused fashion and is not easily manageable. Being an intuitive person, the Strategist has a predilection for exploring possibilities and opportunities for the future, is gifted in planning, and naturally strives to have foresight and avoid obsolescence. The Strategist knows how to get the most out of a specific situation, although he or she may at times be too theoretical for you.

Strategists trust and enjoy their analytical skills more than involving themselves with hands-on operations. At times, they seem to be arguing for argument's sake, but it is through questioning, interaction, and exploration that they gather sufficient data to make up their minds. In a work setting, your Strategist colleagues would rather understand the underlying reasons for an event than deal with the event itself. They may isolate themselves, especially the Introverted ones. They are so self-confident that they seek no mutuality or dependency upon others. Whereas your attitude as an entrepreneur, especially in the social setting, is one of live for today, the Strategist is always living for tomorrow.

For you, it is easy to be charming and diplomatic, but Strategists don't have these gifts. They work at work and work at play, whereas you play at work as well as at play. Nevertheless, a Strategist is a great complement to a Tactical entrepreneur. These individuals thrive on finding ingenious long-term ways to solve complex problems. They marshal available resources, be they financial, material, or human, and strive to make the best use of those resources.

The Complementary Role of the Idealist

The Idealist entrepreneur is perhaps the most difficult for a Tactician entrepreneur to understand and therefore appreciate. You are concrete and pragmatic; the Idealist is more oriented toward abstraction and people. The contribution of an Idealist associate, when provided with the proper environment, is in mentoring and supporting individuals in a humanitarian rather than an operational fashion.

The intangible value provided by such entrepreneurs may constitute the difference between business as usual and becoming a stellar performer. Idealist managers understand human motivation better than any of the other three types of entrepreneur. As a Tactician entrepreneur, you may occasionally work on your people skills, but your Idealist complement naturally creates circumstances whereby people want to work together and deliver their best performance. They are strong supporters of people coming together in a mutually supportive environment and sharing their various skills and expertise in order to exceed expectations.

Your need for feedback is different from your Idealist counterpart. When you've achieved spectacular results, you enjoy the standing ovation, but Idealists need compliments along the way, for they affiliate so much with others that feedback is critical for them to determine if they are on the right track.

Expect an Idealist entrepreneur to be both bruised and hurt by indifference, rejection, and criticism. Unlike Tacticians, who quickly forget, Idealist types have the tendency to burden themselves with negative feedback to the point where their performance declines. Therefore, think about such a partner as providing insight into people and their motivation, a talent you and other entrepreneurs lack.

Idealists express themselves in symbolic language or metaphor in order to reveal a richer and deeper meaning on important issues. Thus they are great complements for Tacticians. The risk is that both of you may be like ships passing in the night.

The Strategist

Assuming you are a reasonably purebred Strategist entrepreneur, you live in a world of concepts, ideas, and possibilities. You are always on the road to some better place, and there is not much around you that is allowed to stagnate. You may tell people you are a team player, but you really are not. That does not mean, however, that you do not play with the team and even identify with the team. Yet you are always fiercely independent. You attempt to understand where everybody is going, and then you run so fast that you pass them all, becoming not only the leader of the pack but eventually also the prophet and visionary guru.

Your Role Perception

As a Strategist, you strive to be an incomparable achiever. You live in the fast lane and are so involved with reasoning and marshaling your scarce resources that there is not much time for anything other than work. Your staunchest competitor is yourself, and you are always focused on possibilities, opportunities, and problems. Indeed, if there are no problems, you easily feel superfluous. Because you spend your life in the future, there are times when you seem aloof and arrogant. You often think, I've been there, done that—is that all I have to contribute?

The Complementary Role of the Tactician

There are Tacticians you admire because at times they have the guts you don't, and they do things with panache and style, albeit sometimes at a higher risk than you are willing to assume. They can be a great asset for you in your entrepreneurial pursuits because they are at their best when the organization is in a crisis. Whereas you tend to position your organization to be a significant player for the long haul, the Tactician deals with the short haul.

It is normal for a Strategist like yourself to take the high road and move in and out of situations based both upon intuition and thought. Your Tactician complement relies upon an ability to pick up on subtle changes and nuances and knows what to do in a pinch—hence, they often take the low road, allowing themselves to be far more concrete and hands-on than you would ever want to be. However, in a working relationship, they need to learn to rely upon your conceptual capabilities so they can direct their energies toward your desired results. Not easy to manage, they require a fair amount of maintenance to stay focused, for they tend to be opportunity driven rather than pursuing agreed-upon strategic plans.

You are likely to take both yourself and life quite seriously, but your Tactician complements understand how to enjoy work. Being tremendously hands-on people, they dislike theorizing and contemplating, even on a one-to-one basis, in staff meetings or other forums. As an entrepreneur, your preoccupation is with "what to be," whereas the Tacticians are far more alert to "what to do." Like you though, Tacticians are likely to respond to impulse and changing circumstances, and they do so spontaneously.

Although the Tactician does not contribute much to your strategic planning process, he or she can be an immense resource in the implementation of heretofore uncharted operations. You need a plan to know where you are going, whereas your Tactician colleague favors the "dropping in" approach to stay abreast of changes and nuances in the work environment. Do not expect your Tactician complement to prepare much for anything but rather to improvise so skillfully that he or she appears to have carefully preplanned.

Although they are great troubleshooters, Tacticians can also get you into trouble if their role is not fully articulated, understood, and adhered to. But for a Strategist such as yourself, a Tactician is like a breath of fresh air. Just make sure that she or he doesn't blow up into a storm.

The Complementary Role of the Administrator

You probably will benefit most from the Administrator type because the Administrator is committed to being the organizer and implementer, representing all the good things you need to make your plans work. For Administrators, words are their bonds, and they apply all of their mental capacities to meet your expectations. However, whereas you can comfortably work off a hunch, an Administrator requires clear directions and guidance. Once directions are articulated, understood, and brought into practice, your fellow Administrator provides both the authority and skills necessary to get the job done. Your great strength is conceptualizing, while the Administrator monitors.

This does not necessarily mean that you will enjoy working with Administrators: To you, they appear to lack imagination and fascination with the unknown. Indeed, they take pride in achieving tangible results. Think about it this way: The Administrator complements you by delivering concrete results while you, the philosopher, are enjoying abstractions and intellectual debate.

Being a Strategist, you tend to experiment in order to learn more about future opportunities, whereas your Administrator counterpart resists dealing with anything that is not known. Hence, while you are comfortable anticipating the future, the Administrator tries to realize the tried and proven. Moreover, your Administrator partner creates a secure, dependable, and predictable work environment for everyone involved, while you, naturally, are out problem hunting.

Administrators enjoy the authority that comes with improving their operational skills, whereas your satisfaction in terms of authority comes with increasing your knowledge base. Typically, Administrators set goals and objectives through job descriptions and provide timely and orderly performance assessment. You are not likely to direct your energy to organizational building; you are too busy conceptually understanding how it all works. Thus, you can leave the implementation and the day-to-day business for the Administrator to worry about. You enjoy masterminding how to derive the highest benefits out of scarce resources; your complementary Administrator makes sure that those resources are utilized in an accountable and responsible fashion.

The Administrator needs to be viewed not as a necessary evil but as a valuable asset in getting the work done both in terms of quantity and quality, opening the way for you to build the future continuously.

The Complementary Role of the Idealist

Whereas both you and the Idealist types rely a great deal upon intuition, your intuition is directed toward achieving results for the organization, and Idealist entrepreneurs use their intuition in understanding how human beings can better collaborate to produce stunning results. Moreover, whereas you tend to be a rugged individualist, your Idealist complement puts effort into establishing rapport with others so they in turn can contribute value to the business. You both have a great ability to work with abstractions, yet the Idealist can perceive you as being uncaring, manipulative, cold, and controlling.

To work with an Idealist entrepreneur can be challenging simply because these individuals are so interested in people that they bring out the very best in them, sometimes at the price of not achieving the results within the time frame you have established. Bear in mind that as a Strategist entrepreneur, you can be so driven by what you want to achieve that you tend to be indifferent to anything that is not a priority. Your Idealist colleague, however, although also wanting spectacular results, prefers to achieve them by bringing about harmonious and mutually supportive work environments. The enthusiasm of Idealists can easily be contagious, and they can become magnificent leaders in creating circumstances that cause performance to soar.

Above all, as a Strategist entrepreneur you tend to be rational. You always seek an explanation for everything. Your Idealist complement, on the other hand, doesn't need to know why things are the way they are because often he or she can use intuition and built-in confidence, acquired from relating with people, to gain insights and understanding. You use intuition mostly for pragmatic reasons and for deriving an understanding of what needs to be done in order to propel your business forward, whereas the Idealist type uses intuition to create an environment where people want to cooperate. An Idealist in an organization in turmoil can ferret out differences and bring people together, establishing healthier interpersonal relations.

Idealists, then, provide intelligent and workable solutions in difficult situations. They have an unusual capability to bond with and understand people, a strength that is often neither understood nor appreciated by you. In the final analysis, the Idealist complement to you as a Strategist entrepreneur is one of creating values to sustain your organization.

The Idealist

Idealist entrepreneurs are distinguished from the other three types by a unique motivation and devotion to people and work. Idealist types probably feel more "called" to assume the leadership role than do other entrepreneurs. Indeed, they may even feel drafted and ordained into their position of providing inspiration for all to achieve the best possible results.

Your Role Perception

In the role of an entrepreneur, you are driven less by material than by spiritual values. Unlike the other entrepreneurial styles, you may not have set out to assume the responsibility of entrepreneurial leadership. You are not likely to view your organization or any structured environment to be of particular value in achieving your goals and dreams. You approach your task with a great deal of idealism and faith, believing mountains can be moved when people come together in fulfilling a vision. You are the consummate harmonizer, always considering people before things. That is not to suggest that you do not enjoy creature comforts. However, you obtain those through and with people who are willing to provide exceptional work products.

You attempt to assume as much responsibility for the well-being and happiness of people as you do for the bottom line. As a matter of fact, your concern with the profitability of your business is at times subordinated to creating the right kind of environment for people. You are also likely to take a personal interest in the lives of people with whom you associate, at times devoting energy to resolve conflicts—you know that if people are not happy they cannot be productive. A gifted listener, you understand people's subtext, and your devotion to those who are important to you is second to none. In fact, there are times when you take difficult, interpersonal, and dramatic information to heart more than anyone else. Discord and non-supportive human interaction can ruin your day. Your success as an entrepreneur, therefore, comes both from your vision to create values and from the people with whom you work and interact.

The Complementary Role of the Administrator

For you, the Administrator is at worst a necessary evil or, far better, the expediter. Without the complement of the judicious Administrators, your organizational climate can be intensely inspirational, but it may sometimes be difficult to get work done on schedule. For you, an Administrator may appear to be a tough taskmaster with neither heart nor soul. You may not understand or quite accept the modus operandi of the Administrator, but it is advantageous to know that whereas you affiliate with people, Administrators are unbendingly loyal to the organization. Hence, both of you are inclined to accept and understand the value of teams, but for different reasons: You focus on people harmoniously supporting one another to complete the task, whereas the Administrator completes the task with or without harmony. Your Administrator complement may appear less aware than you are of people and their needs but can also be caring. However, the obligations and responsibilities of meeting deadlines and expectations usually take precedence.

There is another important difference between the two of you. As an Idealist type, you are exceptionally gifted in having dreams and visions of things to come. Administrators do not have that experience; they can tap into some of your visualizations, but they unconsciously convert them into work, for they are concrete and you are abstract. In addition, you are spiritually oriented, whereas your Administrator partners are preoccupied with meeting deadlines and delivering products and services.

A sense of fulfillment for you as an Idealist entrepreneur comes from the energies and synergies of people working together to achieve extraordinary results, whereas your Administrator partner experiences inner peace and satisfaction when everything is on schedule according to plans and budgets. Thus, under the right circumstances, an Administrator can be instrumental in making your dreams come true. You may derive more satisfaction from working with people like yourself, but when an abstract and a concrete person work well together, there is limitless potential.

The Complementary Role of the Tactician

You may find it difficult to understand and accept the Tactician. A Tactician is unmanageable and requires freedom to roam. Additionally, the Tactician has a narrow focus and a need to deal with things specifically and concretely, in contrast to your visions and long-term thinking. Yet your two styles share a gift for creativity. As an Idealist type, you envision pleasing, supporting, and providing meaning for your customers. You subordinate yourself to the needs of others while quietly and modestly contributing. Tacticians, however, strive to provide aesthetic values that satisfy their own standards, whether or not they are aligned with your expectations, believing that people will eventually appreciate and understand their unique contribution. Working with Tactician partners, therefore, tends to be disorganized and unpredictable, for they trust their impulses—above all, in a pinch.

You may also find Tactician partners more risktaking than you are because they love to do unconventional things. They sometimes succeed and, at other times fail, miserably. Your risktaking is motivated by a vision, whereas theirs comes from the personal satisfaction of making a major impact. Tacticians are natural procrastinators who are unlikely to prepare for much, if anything. Yet in each situation, they trust their ability to meet surprises with flair, instinctively sensing what has to be done. Your tactician colleagues also function well—in fact, shine—in crisis situations. They like a standing ovation; you are satisfied with a warm handshake.

Tactician partners are more interested in the journey and the adventure than in arriving at the goal, although that is not to say that they have no interest in achieving results. However, they derive more satisfaction from participating in the action. Ultimately, they complement you in delivering performance during the most difficult times when others are backing off.

The Complementary Role of the Strategist

The style of a Strategist can favorably affect a situation with an Idealist at the outset. Be aware, however, that a Strategist partner is someone who, although sharing your a capacity for being abstract, is not likely to be especially sensitive to peoples' needs. Strategists are driven by the need to arrive at the future first; thus they are obsessed with formulating strategies to outperform competitors. However, they are not necessarily the greatest implementers and may seem cold, calculating, and insensitive. They seldom accept anything for what it is and by instinct always seek to improve things. Strategists are not bound to convention; therefore their contribution may at times be so far afield as to be dangerously risky.

What you do share with the Strategist is the ability to envision the future because, for different reasons, both of you are dedicated to do today what has to be done to deserve a tomorrow. Both of you are caring: You care about people and their happiness, and the Strategist cares about providing people with goods and services to improve their lives.

Your Strategist partner tends to work with concepts in a systematic and categoric, yet nonlinear, fashion and is fascinated by and responsive to variables.

One of your natural gifts as an Idealist entrepreneur is to be able to discuss issues of importance with others. Your Strategist partners may be somewhat awkward in such discussions because they do not know how to deal with feelings. Their greatest strength is to be involved with the design and the blueprint for the future. Strategists abhor routine and are not very good at it. Their best contribution is to face challenges and resolve problems in theory, without being burdened with the implementation. Workaholics, they are likely to take both themselves and their situation quite seriously. They are always on a crusade to achieve spectacular results as efficiently as possible. In a trouble-free organization, they are likely to become bored and redirect their energies toward other endeavors.

CHAPTER EIGHT

LEADERSHIP

Leadership is not
a matter of technique;
it creates a set of conditions
where people want to do
what needs to be done.
—Unknown

E ntrepreneurs build and sustain their success as a result of their ability to provide a specific kind of leadership appropriate for their unique set of circumstances. Leadership is different from management work: It involves discovering, mobilizing, and evolving the forces that will permanently strengthen an organization and bring it into the future. Strategist and Idealist entrepreneurs contemplate the future, whereas Administrators and Tacticians focus on delivering their goods and services faster, better, and cheaper than any competitor.

Management is a different yet necessary activity. Its goal is to produce products and services providing customers with the best possible value. Think about it this way: Leaders are primarily concerned with being effective, optimizing the strategic benefits of available resources. Managers are focused on being efficient, getting the highest possible productivity from employees and available resources.

Leadership is practiced in many ways depending upon the individual leader's personality. No magic or uniform approach guarantees success. But effective leaders share three traits: (1) they never abandon their sense of purpose; (2) they build trust; and (3) they enable key people to deliver superior performance.

Each one of the four entrepreneurial types approaches his or her obligations differently. Yet the leadership process of each is somewhat predictable. Of course, keep in mind that the stuff entrepreneurs are made of is unique for each individual.

The Administrator

The sense of purpose for Administrators is borne out by the dynamics and the circumstances created by their very own work ethic. As their enterprise grows, their sense of purpose and responsibility expands. Eventually, there may not be enough hours in the day for them to provide the quality of leadership they would like. Administrators' sense of purpose is triggered by multiple pressure points: They have a strong need to meet or exceed customer expectations; they are unbendingly loyal to people and situations they have invested in over time, both as a result of shared growing pains and a natural respect for human dignity; and they cannot let anyone down or compromise their own beliefs.

Administrators build trust, not surprisingly, by assuming responsibility and being predictable in everything they do. They will go to whatever length it takes to fulfill their commitments. Indeed, their work ethic is to underpromise—and overdeliver.

The Tactician

Tactician entrepreneurs derive a sense of purpose from two conditions: First, because Tacticians are motivated by the need for personal freedom, they will search for situations where the payoff and short-term gratification can be absorbed, enjoyed, and consumed. Second, they gravitate toward opportunities to make a personal difference and add value in a hands-on fashion.

Tactical entrepreneurs are never philosophically aloof. The trust they build is based on their innate ability to know what to do before others are even aware of what is happening. Tacticians find amazing solutions in unanticipated crisis situations where others might have given up the ghost. It is particularly rewarding for Tacticians to teach and guide others in becoming more skilled and improving their performance. Honing professional skills, for the Tactician, is a vital activity in enhancing quality along with the ability to deliver and expedite superior work products.

The Strategist

The sense of purpose for Strategists means marshaling all available resources and optimizing current performance to gain strength and provide a solid foundation for the future. This purpose is reflected in their never-ending crusade to arrive at the future before the competition. Indeed, for them, nothing is ever good enough and everything needs improvement.

The trust Strategist entrepreneurs instill in people originates in their can-do, energetic attitude. They can be relied on to seldom, if ever, slow down, give up, or take no for an answer. They will do whatever they can to find a way even under the most adverse circumstances.

Additionally, they thrive on the confidence people place in their analytical and reasoning abilities. Therefore, they can be trusted to always be on the road to some better place. These entrepreneurs place much confidence in people who are self-critical and who challenge their own performance and thus ultimately create more value. They tend to bring out the best in people in a hands-off fashion. However, if and when performance is not up to expectations, or worse, is declining, the Strategist entrepreneur does not shy away from harsh judgments.

The Idealist

Idealists want to be an inspiration for those with whom they work. They have a genuine interest in producing amazing results based on commitment, dedication, and people coming together to be the best they possibly can. Idealists instinctively build strong and deep relationships, both within their organizations and among the customers they serve. Being a resource and catalyst and encouraging people to be high achievers is an everyday activity for these entrepreneurs. The trust Idealists earn is based on their search for authenticity. Their colleagues know that their intent is to build working relationships without second guessing or hidden agendas: With Idealists, what you see is what you get.

Natural-born mentors, Idealists are patient and derive satisfaction from guiding individuals both in their personal and professional growth.

The Ultimate Challenge: Mobilizing Your Entrepreneurial Capabilities

Assume that you have placed yourself in the ultimate challenging position of launching out on your own, joining the ranks of those who create value independent of whatever is currently known and practiced.

Implied in the work of the entrepreneurs discussed in this book, five principles emerge that can guide you in your professional life. Consider and assess these principles in your work situation. They are my gift to you.

▲ Create an environment allowing you to attract, develop, and retain superior performers.

▲ Make sure that environment energizes the employees and encourages pride and commitment to unparalleled personal and professional growth.

▲ Learn to work in boundaryless teams to create superior values.

▲ Allow people to thrive and enjoy themselves in your presence; commit yourself to understanding *their* realities.

▲ Finally, don't be overly preoccupied with beating the competition. Be the only one doing what you do.

Now go for it.

About the Author

Olaf Isachsen, a native-born Norwegian, received his M.B.A. from Harvard and his Ph.D. from Michigan State University. He has served as associate professor and director of the M.B.A. program at California Polytechnic Institute, as visiting professor at the Stanford Graduate School of Business Administration, and as guest lecturer at several universities, including Bringham Young University and the University of Notre Dame.

As a recognized expert in communications within organizations and in the power of the diversity in human relationships, Dr. Isachsen has been a consultant to numerous corporations, such as Bechtel, the Kaiser Companies, Weyerhauser, Olin-American, Hewlett-Packard, Heidrick & Struggles, and Wells Fargo Bank. He has worked for the U.S. and Australian departments of defense, assisting in the development of major defense contracts, and also participated, under the auspices of the United Nations, in the Caribbean Conference on Sustainable Tourism.

As a past participant of the prestigious Jungian Winter Seminar in Switzerland, Dr. Isachsen has applied unconventional insights into how to develop organizations and their people to their fullest potential. Continuing his interest in opening up this fascinating world of human relationships to a wider audience, Dr. Isachsen addresses organizations and conducts seminars throughout the United States and Europe for such noted groups as the Young President's Organization, the American Bankers Association, and the American Society for Training and Development.

A prolific writer, Dr. Isachsen has written case studies on management for Harvard University and has published numerous articles in journals such as the *Journal of Applied Management, Training Magazine, The Journal of Thought*, and *Personnel Administrator*. Other recent publications have focused on leadership style with corporations, corporate life-cycles, innovation, motivation, and strategic planning.

For the past thirteen years, Dr. Isachsen has served as chairman of the board and senior consultant for the Institute for Management Development (IMD) where he has devoted his time and energy to the study of human typology. He has been able to use the insights of Carl Gustav Jung, Isabel Briggs Myers, and David Keirsey to significantly improve the performance of business organizations. As a nationally recognized management consultant, businessman, dynamic public speaker, and respected educator, Dr. Isachsen offers a wide range of services through the offices of IMD.

Index

For Additional Information

Are you interested in learning more about the topics covered in this book? Learning how Dr. Olaf Isachsen can help you or your company with the challenges facing business leaders in managing for the future, or learning how to more effectively manage the people in your organization?

The Institute for Management Development (IMD) offers a wide range of products and services that can help you in your efforts to be more efficient and productive in both your personal and business life.

Please provide us with the information requested below and we will be happy to send you more details.

Name _____

Title _____

Company _____

Address _____

_____

_____

I am interested in learning more about:
- ❐ *Myers-Briggs Type Indicator*® personality inventory
- ❐ Other books on related subjects
- ❐ Organizational Strategic Planning
- ❐ An Organizational Climate Study
- ❐ 360-degree and Peer Evaluations
- ❐ Business Consultation
- ❐ Please add me to the IMD mailing list

Please return this page to:

THE INSTITUTE FOR MANAGEMENT DEVELOPMENT, INC.
31831 Camino Capistrano, Suite 201
San Juan Capistrano, CA 92675

If we can answer any other questions, please call us at (800) 386-0550, or Fax (714) 489-7875.